# Michael Howe

## The Last and Worst
## of the Bushrangers
## of Van Diemen's Land

## &

## The Van Diemen's Land
## Warriors

**GEORGE MACKANESS**

**ETT IMPRINT**
Exile Bay

First published by ETT Imprint, Exile Bay in 2021

Copyright © ETT Imprint 2021

*Michael Howe* was first published by Andrew Bent in 1818
*Van Diemen's Land Warriors* published by Andrew Bent in 1827
New editions published by George Mackaness in 1944 and 1945
included introductions and an essay on Matthew Brady

ETT IMPRINT
PO Box R1906
Royal Exchange NSW 1225 Australia


ISBN 978-1-922698-05-6 (paper)
ISBN 978-1-922698-06-3 (ebook)


Cover image: View of Hobart Town by Joseph Lycett, London 1824

Design by Tom Thompson

# CONTENTS

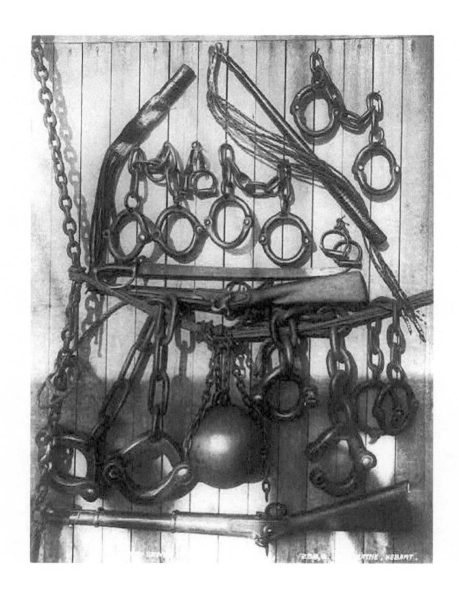

Relics of convict disipline, Hobart.

# INTRODUCTION

## THE AUTHOR

The author of the narrative which is printed in this volume   was Thomas Wells, the "E" which he added to his name having been inserted, it is said, "for family reasons." Early in the nineteenth century, Wells,   a convict, was transported to  New South  Wales, his offence, as set out by Edward Abbott, Junior,  Deputy Judge- Advocate for Tasmania, at the Bigge Inquiry in 1819 , being "Embezzling his employer's funds."

Having been granted a ticket-of-leave, he arrived in Hobart in 1814, where, in April 1816, he was  appointed "the regular established clerk" in the office of the newly arrived Lieutenant-Governor, William Sorell, with whom he apparently  became a great  favourite. It  has been asserted that he was a relative of the Rev . Samuel Marsden. If such a connexion existed,  I have not been able to trace it.

Wells, who is now described as  "a   cultivator  and holder of land," soon began  to speculate.  In 1820  he bought the lease of a town allotment facing Macquarie Street, on which he erected a good house; he secured a grazing licence at Stony Hut Plains, beyond New  Norfolk,  next to the property of his  friend,  an  ex-convict named Brodribb; he purchased from the Government  four  stud rams at seven guineas each. During the Bigge Inquiry, when giving evidence, he told the Commissioner : "I purchased a farm  of  65 acres  at  Newtown  immediately on my arrival; on the following January, I purchased the adjoining farm to it of 75  acres;  afterwards two others adjoining, and sheep in  February,  1818;  I built  a house and  farming  buildings  on  the  first  purchased land. "

Later, he became the owner of the Allandale  Station  in the Hamilton district.

Allegations that the Lieutenant-Governor held shown undue favouritism to Wells by allowing him, a ticket-of- leave man, to submit tenders for the supply of meat from his farms, were investigated by Bigge. That he had done so was definitely proved, for on one occasion he secured a contract for 2000 lbs. of meat for the Government Stores. There was, however, no suggestion of dishonesty; in point of fact, Abbott seems to have been of opinion that he was quite honourable in carrying out his duties. Others, however, complained that he was not always "respectful."

His own evidence before Bigge was restricted almost entirely to questions concerning his professional clerical duties, in particular to his methods of issuing Certificates of Freedom, drawing up of indents, muster rolls, lists or convicts , assignments and licences for occupation.

Wells, who was emancipated in 1819, was, in 1820, a married man with four children, drawing rations, as an official, for himself, his family and two " Government men," labourers on his farm. He seems to have attained some degree of respectability, for we find him recorded as the holder of a reserved pew in St. David's Church, Hobart.

The last official notice of Welt's career is when we find him in 1828 confined in the Debtors' Prison at Hobart, one of his debts being for a sum of £156, incurred in the purchase of certain timber from the Government. The rest is silence.

His book on Michael Howe is derived largely from personal knowledge, aided by Government records, to which he had access. As it is, however, not very accurate, I have thought it wise, in order to give a truer picture, to preface this reprinting of his rare volume with an accurate account of Howe's career based on authentic historical sources.

## THE BOOK

In December, 1818, a small octavo volume of 40 pages, "the first unofficial book or pamphlet printed in Tasmania," to quote the words of Mr. Justice J. A. Ferguson in his Bibliography of Australia, was issued by the well-known Hobart printer, Andrew Bent. It bore the title, *Michael Howe, the last and worst of the Bushrangers of Van Diemen's Land.* The first edition, priced at five shillings, was sold out by June; in July appeared another at half-a-crown.

The pamphlet was reprinted as Appendix No. VII. to *An Account of the Colony of Van Diemen's Land, principally designed for the use of Emigrants,* by Edward Curr (London, 1824), who himself resided in Hobart during the years 1820-1823. Copies of the pamphlet were still being advertised for sale at the office of the Hobart Town Gazette as late as 13th October, 1821.

In 1925, the original manuscript, or the copy of it made for submission to Governor Sorell's censorship, was discovered in Tasmania and reprinted, with a short introduction by Mr. J. H. M. Abbott, by Angus & Robertson of Sydney, in a limited edition of one hundred copies, numbered and signed by the publishers. This is quite unprocurable today.

Of Wells's original editions, only two copies are known. One is in the Bodleian Library, Oxford; the other, purchased in 1897, is in the British Museum. Concerning the latter, Mr. Justice Ferguson has the following note: "It is described in 'Three Hundred Notable Books added to the Library of the British Museum under the Keepership of Richard Garnett, 1890-1899. Edinburgh: printed by T. and A. Constable for the editors and subscribers, 1899." The statement there made at p. 172 that it is the first pamphlet or book printed in Australasia is seriously in error. A considerable number of books and pamphlets had been printed in Sydney prior to 1818. It may, however, be fairly described as the first work of general literature printed in Australasia."

In 1856, a copy of the pamphlet was shown as in the Library of the Royal Society of Tasmania. It cannot now be traced.

The pamphlet was reviewed as a literary curiosity in the *Edinburgh Review* in the year 1820.

On the 30th March, 1819, Lieutenant-Governor Sorell sent a private letter from Hobart to Governor Macquarie enclosing two copies of *The History of Michael Howe's Career*. Neither of these has been discovered.[1]

In the same year it was reviewed in the Quarterly, whose critic observed: "It is the greatest literary curiosity that has come before us-the first child of the press of a State only fifteen years old. It would, of course, be reprinted here; but our copy, *penes nos*, is a genuine Caxton. This little book would assuredly be the *Reynarde Foxe* of Australian bibliomaniacs."

## THE SUBJECT

When in 1852, John West, Minister of St. John Square, Launceston, and first important Tasmanian historian, issued his History of Tasmania, he devoted a sub-section to the career of Michael Howe, his information being derived, as he mentions in a footnote, from the Sydney Gazette, quoted by Wentworth; Commissioner Bigge's Reports; and Bent's [i.e.,Wells's] Life of Howe. West succinctly sets out the lawless conditions which prevailed in the colony at the outset of Howe's long criminal career. He wrote:-

"Towards the close of 1813, the daring and sanguinary violence of bushrangers reduced the colony to the utmost distress; the settlers, generally of the lowest class, received their plunder, and gave them notice of pursuit. Their alliance with stock-keepers, who themselves passed rapidly, and almost naturally, from the margin of civilised to a lawless life, was well understood; nor could they readily refuse their friendship; the government, unable to afford them protection, left them no other source of safety. The division of the colonists into those who had been convicts, and those who controlled them, naturally ranged all of loose principles on the side of the outlaws. Nor was this mode of life without attractions; they were free; their daring seemed like heroism to those in bondage. They not infrequently professed to punish severity to the prisoners, and like Robin Hood of old, to pillage the rich that they might be generous to the poor. The course adopted by the government indicated the strength of the robbers: despairing to reduce them by force, in 1814 Macquarie tendered pardon, except for the crime of murder, to those who, within six months, should return to their duty. To give effect to this treaty, time was judged necessary for its publication; and to allow for the hesitation of the penitent, a distant day was appointed for closing the door.[2]"

This singular document was prepared by his Majesty's judge who was thus himself bound in honour to its unexampled conditions; but the legal acumen of the robbers soon detected the error: its effect was not only pardon for the past, but, with the exception of murder, a license to ravage the colony until the date expired. Thus, they gathered the harvest of crime, and continued their depredations to the last. Nor was another advantage foreseen, although eagerly embraced by the robbers: they almost universally submitted, and having cleared with the law, were prepared again to abscond, and risk once more the chances of the field; but if the document was absurd, the conduct of the local authorities was not less impolitic.

The removal of the men, so well acquainted with the colony and its hundred retreats, was an obvious, yet neglected, precaution: some were satisfied with their past experience, but others lost no time in returning to the bush.[3]

Such was the state of Tasmania when the notorious Michael Howe first began to come into the limelight. In order to place the salient facts of his career before the reader, the following brief account, based principally on the *Historical Records of Australia*, will serve as a prelude to Wells's Narrative.

A Yorkshireman, born in 1787 at Pontefract, Michael Howe was apprenticed in youth aboard a merchant vessel sailing out of Hull, but after two years of service ran away to join a man-of-war, from which a little later he deserted. Afterwards he owned and ran a small coal craft. Arrested in 1811 on a charge of highway robbery, he was convicted and sentenced to seven years' transportation to Van Diemen's Land. He reached Hobart in the convict transport Indefatigable on 19th October,

1812, and was assigned to the service of a prominent merchant and stockholder named Ingle, a former superintendent of convicts, whose character, according to Macquarie and Davey, was none too good.

Under the pretence that having served his King he would be no man's slave, Howe escaped to the bush and joined a gang of bushrangers which had been formed as far back as 1810 by John Whitehead, and at one time numbered as many as twenty-eight members, amongst whom were a deserter from the 73rd Regiment and two aboriginal women.

When in 1814 Macquarie proclaimed his amnesty, it is said that Howe came in with the rest, but was out again within a month or two, taking the opportunity to raid a farm belonging to his former master, Ingle, only twelve miles distant from Hobart.

There are different stories concerning the fate of Whitehead. According to Wells, whose story is repeated by West, he and Howe had agreed that, if either was killed in a fight with the police, the survivor should cut off the dead man's head to prevent the pursuers from getting the reward; that Whitehead was killed in such a fight about the middle of May, 1815, and that Howe did what he had promised; but that the head was afterwards found, and the body gibbeted on Hunter's Island. In September, 1815, however, William Stewart, master of the merchant sloop Fly, reported to the Colonial Secretary at Sydney that several bushrangers, including Whitehead, had been taken off by a whaleboat to one of the islands in Bass Strait, and were raiding the seal fisheries there.[4]

By the end of 1815 Howe was the acknowledged leader of the gang, upon whom he imposed a discipline almost naval in its severity. As West asserts: "They subscribed to articles, which bound them to obedience; penalties were inflicted, such as cutting and carrying wood for their fires, or even stripes. He professed the piety of a quarter-deck, and read to them the Scriptures." By 1816 he was signing himself "Lieutenant-Governor of the Woods," and in 1817 "Governor of the Ranges."

Incredible as it may appear, Howe corresponded both with Sorell and Davey as though he were their equal. That letters should pass between the administrator of the Government and men living in open defiance of law and order affords a strange commentary on the state of society at this period. On one occasion, before sending to the Governor a letter signed by himself and ten others of the gang, he made them swear on an Anglican Prayer Book to abide by its terms.

On 14th December, 1817, Lieutenant-Governor Thomas Davey transmitted to the Earl of Harrowby a copy of Macquarie's Proclamation concerning the bushrangers, dated 14th May, 1814, together with a letter to himself from the bushrangers "written in blood," together with his (Davey's) answer, dated 30th November, 1816. Here is the letter, as priceless a piece of effrontery as can be imagined:-

### LETTER FROM THE BUSHRANGERS
### TO LIEUTENANT- GOVERNOR DAVEY.

"From the Bushrangers to the Honor'ble T. Davey, Lieutenant Governor of Van damand's Land. Sir, We have Thought proper to write these Lines To You As we have Been Kept In the Dark so long And We find it his Only to Keep Us Quiet Untill By some Means or another you think you can get Us Betrayed. But We will stand it No Longer We Are Now Determined to have it full and Satisfactory Either for or Against Us So We are Determined to Be Kept No Longer In Ignorance for We think Ourselves Greatly Injured By the Country At large In lay in To Hour Charge that Horid An detestable crime which We have fully Satisfied the Eyes of the Publick In All our Actions To the Contrary During our Absence from the Settlement I Have not the least Doubt But you are glad that these New Hands joining Us We Are Glad Also though you think I Dare Say They Will prove to Our Disadvantage And We think to the Contrary And He who Preserved Us from your Plots in Publick will Likewise Preserve Us from them in Secret as We Are not Unacquainted with you having A party in Secret and Likewise Where they are And where We as much Inclined to take Life As you Are in your Hearts We Could Destroy All the Partyes you Can send out And Without We Have A Little Quietness More than What We have Had you shall soon Be Convinced of What I say. Therefore if you Wish to prevent it Send Word out By Bearer Richard Westlick Which We Expect To Return on the 9th of the Ensuing Month With An Answer To Us Do not think to Defraud Us By sending out a party on this head for if you do you Take Away the Man's Life if they Are Either With him Or Watching him for We Will Be Watching Likewise you Must Not think to Catch Hold Birds With Chaff. Therefore To Affirm the Answer Either for Or Against Us that We will Receive Clap on it the King's Seal And Your Signature We have Weighed Well Within Our Own Brests the Consequence Which Will Attend to those Circumstances Therefore I Would Have you Do the same for the Good of the Peacable And Well Disposed Inhabitants of the Territorys of this Land. No More At Present.

MICHL HOWE
JAS GARRY
PETER SEPTON
GEO. JONES X
RICH. COLIER X
JOHN CHAPMAN

THOMAS COYNE
JAMES PARKER
MATHEW KEGAN X
JOHN BROWN X
NENIS CURRY X

To this letter Davey replied on the 30th November:
"Government House, Hobart town.

" The power of Pardoning Capital Offences rests solely with the Governor-in-Chief, but no application for favor

an avail those, who are in the daily Commission of the greatest outrages; Good Conduct is the surest way to Favor.

"T. DAVEY,

"To All whom it may Concern."[5]

Towards the end of Davey's term began a steady process of hunting down the gangs, an aboriginal girl known as Black Mary, who had been Howe's companion since 1814, attended by some brutality of his, offering to guide the police to his haunts. Consequently on 28th April, 1817, a constable from the country brought to Sorell, who had just succeeded Davey, a letter from Howe,[6] a copy of which, with some extracts from Howe's depositions, Sorell sent to Macquarie, but which is, unfortunately, not now available. When Howe surrendered, Sorell granted him a conditional pardon for all crimes except murder, and promised to obtain, if possible, the King's mercy even for murders, provided that Howe made a full confession and betrayed his companions. Howe was examined frequently by the magistrates, his depositions being described as "voluminous and tedious," but no confession was forthcoming. For some reason, Howe endeavoured to implicate the chaplain, the Rev. Robert Knopwood, by accusing him of "an improper intercourse with people living in the woods," charges of which later he was proved incontestably innocent.

When in September 1817, Howe disappeared again, Macquarie revoked the pardon with the comment that "if ever taken alive he will be a very fit and proper object to make a Public and awful example of." [7]

In April, 1818, a Government launch was stolen by a gang of prisoners whose intention it was to pick up Howe and put him aboard an American vessel, but the plan miscarried. Thenceforward Howe was a lone wolf and in constant danger, for Sorell had offered, besides the pecuniary reward, freedom and a passage to England to any prisoner who might succeed in capturing him. In September 1818, a party, including the New South Wales black-tracker, Mosquito, took from him his pistols and a knapsack in which was found his "Journal of Dreams," a little book made of kangaroo skin with the writing in kangaroo's blood. He continued at large until 21st October, when he was killed in a fierce encounter with a soldier named William Pugh and a convict servant, Thomas Worrall. West, in a footnote, paints a vivid story of the capture of Howe, as set down by Worrall some years later in "The Military Sketch Book,"  This is the note :-

"He [Worrall] was entrapped into the Mutiny of the Nore, but the only part which he took in the proceedings, was writing out in a fair hand several papers for the mutineers; and this he declared he did for no other purpose than to indulge his vanity, in displaying his fine writing, upon which he had highly valued himself. He was tried after the surrender of the mutineers, and transported to Van Diemen's Land. 'I was now,' said he, 'determined to make a push for the capture of this villain, Mick Howe, for which I was promised a passage to England in the next ship that sailed, and the amount of the reward laid upon his head. I found out a man of the name of Warburton, who was in the habit of hunting kangaroos for their skins, and who had frequently met Howe during his excursions, and sometimes furnished him with ammunition. He gave me such an account of Howe 's habits, that I felt convinced we could take him with a little assistance. I therefore spoke to a man of the name of Pugh, belonging to the 48th regiment - one whom I knew was a most cool and resolute fellow. He immediately entered into my views, and having applied to Major Bell, his commanding officer, he was recommended by him to the Governor, by whom I was permitted to act, and allowed to join us; so he and I went directly to Warburton, who heartily entered into the scheme, and all things were arranged for putting it into execution. The plan was this: Pugh and I were to remain in Warburton's hut, while Warburton himself was to fall into Howe's way. The hut was on the river Shannon, standing so completely by itself, and so out of the track of anybody who might be feared by Howe, that there was every probability of accomplishing our wishes, and "scotch the snake"- as they say, if not kill it.

'"Pugh and I accordingly proceeded to the appointed hut; we arrived there before daybreak, and having made a hearty breakfast, Warburton set out to seek Howe. He took no arms with him, in order to still more effectually carry his point; but Pugh and I were provided with muskets and pistols. The sun had been just an hour up, when we saw Warburton and Howe upon the top of a hill, coming towards the hut. We expected that they would be with us in a quarter of an hour, and so we sat down upon the trunk of a tree inside the hut, calmly waiting their arrival. An hour passed, but they did not come, so I crept to the door cautiously and peeped out – there I saw them standing, within a hundred yards of us, in earnest conversation; as I learned afterwards, the delay arose from Howe's suspecting that all was not right. I drew back from the door to my station, and in about ten minutes after this we plainly heard footsteps, and the voice of Warburton; another moment, and Howe slowly entered the hut – his gun presented and cocked. The instant he espied us, he cried out, "Is that your game!"– and immediately fired; but Pugh 's activity prevented the shot from taking effect, for he knocked the gun aside. Howe ran off like a wolf. I fired but missed. Pugh then halted and took aim at him, but also missed. I immediately flung away the gun and ran after Howe. Pugh also pursued; Warburton was a considerable distance away. I ran very fast – so did Howe; and if he had not fallen down an unexpected bank, I should not have been fleet enough for him. This fall, however, brought me up with him; he was on his legs, and preparing to climb a broken bank, which would have given him a free run into the wood, when I presented my pistol at him, and desired him to stand; he drew forth another, but did not level it at me. We were about fifteen yards from each other – the bank he fell from between us. He stared at me with astonishment, and to tell you the truth, I was a little astonished at him, for he was covered with patches of kangaroo skins, and wore a black beard – a haversack and powder horn slung across his shoulders. I wore my beard also – as I do now: and a curious pair we looked like.

"After a moment's pause, he cried out, "Black beard against grey beard for a million!"– and fired. I slapped at him, and I believe hit him, for her staggered; but rallied again, and was clearing the bank between him and me, when Pugh ran up, and with the butt end of his firelock knocked him down again, jumped after him, and battered his brains out, just as he was opening a clasp knife to defend himself.'"

On the recommendation of Sorell, Macquarie granted his discharge from the Army to Pugh, and an absolute pardon to Worrall, because, as Sorell said: "Since the murder of G. Watts and Drew some months ago, from whom Howe effected his escape, I am satisfied there are not many people in the Settlement who would have risked the encounter."

# MICHAEL HOWE,

## THE LAST AND WORST OF

## **The Bush Rangers**

### OF

## VAN DIEMEN'S LAND

*

## NARRATIVE OF THE

## CHIEF ATROCITIES COMMITTED BY THIS

## **Great Murderer**

## AND HIS ASSOCIATES

### DURING A PERIOD OF SIX YEARS

## IN VAN DIEMEN's LAND.

### FROM AUTHENTIC SOURCES OF INFORMATION

## HOBART TOWN

### PRINTED BY ANDREW BENT

The Fate of MICHAEL HOWE, and his Confederates in Robbery and Murder, having excited considerable interest in this Colony, the Compiler is induced to offer to the Public the following Narrative of their chief Atrocities, and Particulars of the Extinction of Bush-Ranging in the Death of HOWE;— and as it forms the first Pamphlet from a very confined Press, the Editor claims for it the indulgent Consideration of his Readers, -

Hobart Town,
Van Diemen's Land,
December, 1818,

MICHAEL HOWE, who acted the principal part in the transactions about to be narrated, was born at Pontefract in Yorkshire in the year 1787, and was bound apprentice to a merchant vessel at Hull; but he served only two years when he ran away and entered on board a man-of-war.

In the year 1811 he was apprehended for robbing a miller on the highway, and tried at the York assizes following; but, from an informality in the indictment, the capital part of the charge was abandoned, and he received sentence of seven years transportation : he arrived at this Settlement in the ship *Indefatigable*, Captain Cross, in the month of October 1812,

During his passage from England his habits were rather industrious, and, though always mischievously inclined, he exhibited, no symptoms of that daring and wanton conduct which manifested itself in his future life, unless we may consider as such his leaping overboard, whilst the vessel was in port, and swimming a considerable distance before he was taken.

As a leader of a band of desperadoes, Howe may not unaptly be compared to Three-fingered Jack, who was so long the terror of the peaceable fettlers in the plantations of Jamaica; and who, notwithstanding every exertion to take him, long ranged the woods of that Island, committing the most cruel and daring acts of murder and robbery, until, from the large rewards offered by Government, he was arrested by the hands of justice.

Howe was only a few days at Government public labor before he was assigned, as a crown servant, to Mr. Ingle, a merchant and grazier; from whose service he eloped into the woods, and joined twenty-eight felons at that time at large committing depredations.

With a view of inducing those deluded people to return to their duty to Government, His Excellency Governor Macquarie, on the 14th of May 1814, was pleased to extend to them the Royal Clemency for all offences committed during their unlawful absence (the crime of wilful murder provided they should return to their lawful occupations by the 1st day of December following; denouncing all who should neglect to do so as out-laws.

This banditti, now consisting of twenty-nine persons, amongst whom were Michael Howe and John Whitehead, an equally desperate offender, availed themselves of the proffered clemency, and surrendered to Government.

Although Howe and his companions must at this period have been sensibie that their lives would have been forfeit to the Laws but for the mercy extended to them, this reflection did not operate to amend their future conduct; for we soon after find Howe and Whitehead again in the woods with a new set of desperadoes, adding murder to robbery.

After some minor depredations, this band, headed by Whitehead, stripped nearly the whole of the settlers at New Norfolk of their portable property, together with all arms and ammunition; and from thence proceeded to Pitt Water and robbed Mr. Fisk, a new settler at that place.

In the night of March 10th, they set fire to the wheat-stacks, barns, &c. of A. W. H. Humphrey, Esq. Police Magistrate, and of Bartholomew Reardon, district constable, at Pitt Water, within a few minutes of each other, destroying the produce of one hundred acres recently got in. A paper was found near the burnt stacks of Mr, Humphrey, upon which were words of threatening Import, and the representation of a gun firing a ball at the head of a man.

It afterwards came out that Whitehead and Garland were the principal incendiaries in this wanton destruction.

On the 25th of April 1815, the band, confiding of John Whitehead, the leader, Richard McGuire, Hugh Burne, Richard Collier, Peter Septon, John Jones, James Geary, a deserter from the 73d regiment, and Howe, accompanied by a black native girl named Mary, with whom Howe cohabited, again appeared at New Norfolk, and robbed the house of Mr Carlisle, a settler there, who immediately communicated the circumstance to his neighbour Mr McCarty.

The latter being apprehensive for the safety of his schooner the Geordy, lying near in the Derwent with valuable property, determined to meet the robbers; and, accompanied by several persons on the spot, who immediately volunteered, commenced a pursuit.

Mr. McCarty's party, consisting of himself, Mr. Jemott, Mr. James O'Birne, master of the Geordy, Keith Hacking, mate, Messrs. Carlisle, Murphy, James Triffit, John Brown, and − Tooms, armed with fowling-pieces and pistols, soon came up with the robbers and commanded them to surrender their arms; the gang instantly commenced firing under cover of, and through a large hollow tree, and wounded five of the party, who had the disadvantage of being fully exposed to the fire of the former on every attempt to get a shot at them. Carlisle received a ball in the groin and three slugs in the breast, of which wounds he died within an hour. Mr. Jemott was badly wounded by a ball passing through the thick part of the thigh, in which part Triffit was also wounded, and Murphy in the abdomen. O'Birne received a ball in the cheek, which perforated the tongue and lodged in the neck, causing his death in a few days. The banditti, availing themselves of the disabled state of Mr. McCarty's party, in turn demanded him to lay down his arms, which was refused, and a slight firing continued until the wounded were removed, with the exception of Murphy, whose state obliged him to remain at the mercy of the gang; and they were about to add corporal punishment to their victory, but were prevented by their leader Whitehead.

In consequence of these murders, military parties were sent in various directions in search of the banditti. A party of the 73d regiment in a few days came so close up with them as to find the remains of their fires, and the skin of a sheep recently killed. A party of the 46th was also in pursuit, and a number of the inhabitants of Hobart Town, well-armed, went in search of the murderers of Carlisle and O'Birne.

Lieutenant Governor Davey adopted measures for their apprehension.

EARLY VIEW OF HOBART TOWN.

HOBART TOWN GAOL AND CHAIN GANG.

Hobart scenes, 1819.

A Proclamation had previously to this been published, offering a reward of fifty guineas to any person, free or bond, who would apprehend a bush-ranger, and lodge him in safe custody; holding out encouraging prospects to such of the offenders themselves (not personally implicated in any act of felony) as should procure the apprehension of any of their associates; and it having been represented that the bush-rangers derived supplies from settlers and other fixed inhabitants, a further reward of fifty guineas was offered to any person giving information of such abettors; for without secret assistance these depredations could not long have continued.

On the 10th of May, the band of robbers visited the house of Mr. Humphrey at Pitt Water for the second time. About eleven o'clock in the evening. Whitehead, Septon, and Collier, all armed, burst open the door of the servants' hut and rushed in. Whitehead and Septon immediately presented their muskets cocked to the servants present, and flood over them, whist Collier made them take off their neck-cloths, with which he tied their hands across behind their backs; Whitehead and Septon threatening to shoot them if they resisted or stirred. Howe then came in, and taking a lamp from the hut went, with others who had remained outside, to the dwelling-house occupied by Mr. Humphrey, which they broke open and plundered, while Whitehead, Septon, and Collier stood guard over the servants.

After packing up everything they found useful to themselves, and breaking and destroying what they could not take away (which last they said they should have spared had they not perceived two pair of irons in the house), they departed, threatening if any one stirred out of the hut that he should be shot by sentries which they would place to look out, whist the others might get a sufficient distance.

The banditti shortly afterwards revisited New Norfolk. Knowing Mr. McCarty was absent, and meditating revenge for the opposition met with in their late encounter, they repaired to his premises by night, and wantonly fired a volley in at the window. It happily did no other injury than slightly wounding one soldier. On this occasion they met with an unexpected reception; for a party of the 46th regiment, who had been stationed in the house, immediately commenced a brisk fire, which killed their leader Whitehead.

The party then rushed from the house to cut off the retreat of the banditti, but from the darkness of the night were unable to do so,

When Whitehead received the fatal shot he ran a few yards towards Howe, crying "take my watch, take my watch," and then dropped. Howe immediately took off his head as well perhaps to prevent the body being recognized by their pursuers as in performance of an engagement which they had made to each other, that, upon any one of them being killed, a survivor should do this, to prevent, as they said, any person from benefiting by rewards for taking in their heads.

The head of Whitehead was a considerable time afterwards found in the woods: the body was brought to Hobart Town and gibbeted on Hunter's Island.

From this period Howe was considered the leader of the band.

In the early part of this year Lieutenant Governor established Martial Law in the Colony; which was kept in force till repealed by order of Governor Macquarie; soon after which, a party in quest of the banditti, in the neighbourhood of Tea-tree Brush, described their place of retreat from a smoke which they had made. Near the hut from which it proceeded, were McGuire and Burne (the rest being absent), who immediately darted into a thicket and disappeared, eluding all search.

In the hut was found a number of articles belonging to various individuals whom they had, at different periods, plundered; besides ammunition, musket balls, fire-arms, and several kangaroo dogs.

This discovery caused the reparation of McGuire and Burne from the rest of the banditti, and their speedier fall; for after wandering several days in the woods they applied to a settler, near Kangaroo Point, to procure them a boat for the purpose of proceeding to Bass' Straits; for which service they promised the reward of a watch.

The settler pretended to come into their views, and left them with the assurance of going in search of the boat; but he privately repaired to Hobart Town, and informed the Lieutenant Governor of their intentions. A party of the 46th regiment was immediately dispatched, who surrounded the place of their concealment, and captured both. Burne was the most aged of the gang, and was severely wounded in endeavouring to escape from the party. They were brought before a General Court Martial, charged with being two of the banditti who murdered the unfortunate Cariisle, were convicted, and received sentence of death. They were accordingly executed and their bodies gibbeted on Hunter's Island, near to that of Whitehead, their leader when that murder was committed.

The banditti were now reduced to Howe, Septon, Jones, Geary, and Collier.

From the information of one of the gang, who had been taken in the woods and afterwards admitted an evidence for the crown, a discovery took place of some of the abettors of the bush-rangers in the robbery of Mr. Fisk; in consequence of which, William Stevens, a crown prisoner, and two youths born of European parents at Norfolk Island (who were stock-keepers near to the place where the robbery was committed, and m whose possession some of the stolen property was found), were all apprehended as being concerned with the bush-rangers in that robbery; of which they were afterwards convicted by a General Court Martial, and sentenced to death. Stevens was executed, and the two youths respited under the gallows, which was fixed near to the gibbets on Hunter's lsland; and the body of Stevens was buried within a few yards of the same place.

In October following Martial Law was repealed by order of His Excellency the Governor in Chief.

These awful examples had no tendency to correct the vicious course of the remaining hardened offenders. They committed many acts of plunder in the September following; — they robbed the house of Mr. Stanfield, at Green Point, of every moveable; — they also rushed into the house of Stynes and Troy, settlers at the Plains of the Coal River, and with horrid menaces commanded every person to remain quiet in the dwelling, while they rifled it of every portable article; and a tradesman who at work on the premises, and who some time before had been of the party in pursuit of them, narrowly escaped being shot.

After this month they retired again to the woods, and were not heard of till the 7th of November; when they assailed the residence of David Rofe, Esq. at Port Dalrymple. Their conduct while plundering here was aggravated, as on other occasions, by every wanton atrocity.

Upon this, the Commandant repaired to the woods in person, accompanied by a strong party of the 46th regiment, and the chief constable; they searched the interior of the country several days, but were unable to come up with any of the gang.

These miscreants were next visible at the farm of Mr. T. Hayes, at Bagdad, within eleven days, and at the distance of 100 miles from the scene of their last outrage. Mr. William T. Stocker, a person in the habit of trading between the Settlements, had halted at Hayes's for the night with a cart load of property of great value; the whole of which the banditti forcibly carried off. It is to be supposed that they had previously been informed of Mr. Stocker's journey.

The property taken from individuals by this lawless gang must by this time have been immense; and it is not to be conceived how it was appropriated but by their having confederates in society, though unsuspected, who not only purchased their booty, but were channels of information as to the passing events in which they were interested: and, indeed, we may safely ascribe the long period in which they eluded every exertion made to capture them to this secret support.

Soon after this, the banditti, increasing in hardihood in proportion with the number of atrocities as yet committed with impunity, assumed a lofty tone, and addressed a letter to Lieutenant Governor Davey, replete with ignorant and insolent threats. They, however, complained of being much harrassed by the pursuing parties from the Settlements, and the perseverance used to take them. In addition to the old gang, the letter was signed by six felons, who had lately absconded, named Chapman, Coine, Parker, Keegan, Brown, and Currie. Two native black girls, armed as well as the men, accompanied them.

At this period a most vigilant and persevering search was continued in all directions by parties of military from Hobart Town and Port Dalrymple. Captain Nairn headed a detachment of 20 privates of the 46th regiment, and continued an indefatigable pursuit, night and day. All efforts, however, were as yet unavailing.

The following information, taken before A. W. H. Humphrey, Esq. Justice of Peace, as it shews their state of feeling, and having reference to the letter sent to Lieutenant Governor Davey, may be perused with some interest: —

"John Yorke being duly sworn states, about 5 o'clock in the evening of November 27th, I fell in with a party of bush-rangers, about 14 men and 2 women; Michael Howe and Geary were the only two of the gang I knew personally. I met them on Scantling's Plains— l was on horseback ; they desired me to stop, which I accordingly did on the high road; it was Geary that stopped me; he said he wanted me to see every man sworn to abide by the contents of a letter.—l observed a thick man writing, as I suppose to the Lieutenant Governor. — Geary was the man who administered the oath on a prayer book, calling each man for that purpose regularly: they did not inform me the contents of the letter.— Michael Howe and Geary directed me to state when I came to town the whole I had seen, and to inform Mr. Humphrey (Police Magistrate) and

Mr. Wade (Chief Constable) to take care of themselves, as they were to take their lives, and to prevent them from keeping stock or grain, unless there was something done for them; that Mr. Humphrey might reap what grain he liked, but they would thrash more in one night than he could reap in a year. They said they could set the whole country in a fire with one stick. I was detained about three quarters of an hour, during which time they charged me to be strict in making known what they said to me, and what I had seen. On my returning from Port Dalrymple I called at a hut occupied by Joseph Wright, at Scantling's Plains:—William Williams and a youth were there, who told me the bush-rangers had been there a few days before, and forced them to a place called Murderer's Plains (which the bush-rangers called the Tallow Chandler's Shop), where they made them remain three days, for the purpose of rendering down a large quantity of beef fat, which Williams understood was taken from cattle belonging to Stynes and Troy (these people had lost 150 head of cattle)."

On the 25th of February following, the Commandant of Port Dalrymple sent out Ensign Mahon and a party of the 46th regiment, in pursuit of bush-rangers; and after several weeks in the woods they fell in with Chapman, Parker and Elliott, lying in ambuscade at York Plains. On being called upon to surrender, Chapman snapped his musket at the guide, and with the rest ran off. Three of the soldiers then fired; Chapman was shot through the back, and soon after expired; Parker was slightly wounded, but fled into a thicket and Elliott was shot by Ensign Mahon, and died instantly. The heads of Chapman and Elliott were taken off and sent into Launceston, and the bodies interred on the spot. Parker was afterwards apprehended near the same place in a wretched state.

In the early part of March it appears that some jealousy of Howe began to manifest itself in the old gang; —they conceived, from the circumstance of his being absent at intervals without their knowledge, or assigning any reason, that he meditated betraying the rest. Howe was aware of their suspicions, and, feeling no longer secure among them, suddenly eloped, taking with him the native girl before mentioned.

In April 1817, Lieutenant Governor Sorell arrived, and assumed the government of the Settlements on Van Diemen's Land; and about this period Howe and the native girl were pursued in the neighbourhood of Jericho, by a small party of the 46th regiment.

His wantonly cruel disposition was strongly manifested on this occasion; for being hard pressed, in order to facilitate his own escape, he fired at this poor female companion, who from fatigue was unable to keep pace with him. She received, however, little injury, and together with his blunderbuss, knapsack, and dogs, fell into the hands of the pursuers.

This native girl afterwards became particularly valuable as a guide to the military parties, from the quickness and fagacity peculiar to the black natives in tracing foot-steps where Europeans would not suspect them. She led the party first to some of the places of the banditti's resort at the River Shannon. While employed in burning their huts in this quarter, Jones, Septon, and Geary were seen at the other side of the river: the appearance of the military party, however, gave them no alarm, as they knew the river could not be immediately crossed; the banditti had therefore another opportunity of escape.

Continuing their search, the soldiers next met with 50 sheep in a remote place, stolen from Mr. Stanfield, and concealed by the bush-rangers for future supply.

After the loss of his knapsack and dogs, his confirmed breach with the rest of the banditti, and his late narrow escape, Howe, now entirely alone, appears to have determined upon carrying into execution a design which, according to the report of the native girl, he had for some time contemplated, viz. that of chancing an extension of mercy upon surrender.

He accordingly found means to convey to Lieutenant Governor Sorell a letter offering to give himself up to an Officer, as well as to furnish important information of the friends and  supporters of the old gang, and become the means of their final capture, upon His Honor's assurance of present personal safety, and a favorable representation to His Excellency the Governor in Chief with a request for pardon. The Lieutenant Governor immediately dispatched Captain Nairn, of the 46th regiment, to a place named, with an assurance to that effect; and this Officer on the 29th of April conveyed Howe to Hobart Town, and lodged him in the county gaol. He now underwent various examinations by the Magistrates.

In the meantime the military parties remained in pursuit of the robbers still at large.

On the 10th of May, the party commanded by Serjeant McCarthy arrived in Hobart Town, after an arduous and persevering pursuit under circumstances of peculiar hardship and privation: they had procured information of, and tracked the banditti for several days, until the loss of their flour in fording a river, and a total want of provisions, which reduced them to eat the skin mocassons (kangaroo skin, used instead of shoes) from their feet, compelled them to give up the pursuit for a time.

On the 19th of the same month, the party stationed at Pitt Water, commanded by Lieutenant Nunn, received intelligence that the banditti were robbing the premises of Edward Lord, Esq. at Orielton Park. They hastened to the spot; and on their appearance the banditti fired several shots, and slightly wounded Lieutenant Nunn. Some soldiers, stationed at another part of the Settlement were now seen by the bush-rangers approaching; upon which the latter fled, leaving behind them some flour which they had stolen from Mr. Lord.

About the latter end of June, the Government long boat, employed on the Port Dalrymple river in carrying provisions between George Town and Launceston, was carried away by the bush-rangers, with five more men and several stand of arms; but in consequence of bad weather their design of escaping to the Islands was frustrated; and they were compelled to return. After burning the boat and other articles they were driven again to resume their former habits in the woods.

The old gang might now be considered to have received considerable accession; the number at large having amounted to twenty, in the absence, at this period, of the Lieutenant Governor at the other Settlement.

On the 5th July, a meeting of the principal inhabitants of Hobart Town was held, under the sanction of His Honor, in order to facilitate the views of Government, by raising a sum of money to be applied in rewards for apprehending the banditti then at large; when five hundred and twenty guineas were immediately subscribed.

Upon the result of this meeting, and the recent intelligence of the plunder and excesses at George Town, the Lieutenant Governor issued a Proclamation, holding out the rewards for the apprehension of the old gang :

For Geary . . . . One hundred guineas:

Septon . . . .>

Jones . . . . > Eighty guineas each;

Collier . . . .>

Browne . . . . > Fifty guineas each;

Coine . . . .>

And at the same time was offered, a reward of 80 guineas for George Watts, an old and mischievous bush-robber under colonial Sentence to Hunter's River, but who had only associated with Garland (also an offender in the woods, and who was engaged with Whitehead in burning the stacks at Pitt Water), supposed to be drowned in an attempt to cross the Derwent.

Two days after this Proclamation, the banditti appeared at the Black Brush, and on the following day were traced by Serjeant McCarthy's party to a settler s house at the Tea-tree Brush, where they had dined. On perceiving the military, they ran out of the house and posted themselves behind trees, where the timber on the ground was very thick. An attack commenced on both sides, and though the banditti had certainly the advantage of position, Geary, their leader, by a well-directed fire, was wounded, and fell: he died the same night. Smith and Tull, runaways from Port Dalrymple, who had joined the gang only a few days, were also wounded and taken.

This success would doubtless have been followed up by greater, in the military party, but from its laboring under the disadvantage of great fatigue, from incessant pursuit, and that of a heavy rain which prevented their muskets from going off. The whole of the knapsacks and dogs of the banditti, however, fell into their hands; and it ought to be noted that this little party were at the moment totally unacquainted with the recent Proclamation and offered rewards from the latter of which they were, however, not allowed to remain long without benefiting.

In the mean time Howe continued at the gaol of Hobart Town; but His Excellency the Governor in Chief having received favorably the request made by the Lieutenant Governor, in pursuance of the terms of Howe's surrender, he could not altogether be considered a prisoner for close confinement; upon which account, and his health being reported to be much impaired, he was occasionally permitted to walk out in charge of a constable.

His examinations by the Magistrates were frequent, and his depositions voluminous and tedious; but notwithstanding his promise of a full disclosure of the supporters of the bush-rangers, little information of worth or utility could be gained from him.

It might have been expected that Howe would, at this period, have placed some value on his improved situation being in fact considered a pardoned offender, to whom was afforded a last chance of atoning in some degree for his past crimes by an amended life; and having the prospect of speedily returning to society: but a life of crime obtained with Howe a preference to all others; and on the 26th of July, by some means eluding the vigilance of the constable, to whose care he was entrusted, he again escaped to the woods.

He now felt himself too much a traitor and a villain for the safe admission of a companion or confederate, and never after joined his old associates. He had, indeed, before him a well-founded apprehension of the consequences of his treachery, even from those stamped with similar crimes, should he be found once more in their power.

Thus we find the crimes of this man lead him on, step by step, till he is reduced to prefer the desperate situation of standing opposed to all mankind; compelled unceasingly to watch for his life; certain of feeing an enemy in every human face; certain that to suffer himself for a moment to sleep might terminate his miserable existence; certain, too, that in that deep his enormities would at least visit him with horrid retrospective visions, anticipations of torture, despair, and death; and certain that reality promised no other end :—preferring all these, to the opportunity given him of a life of penitence, and a death at all events not hastened by the hands of justice.

Let us now turn to his old associates in guilt, whom justice seemed to be quickly overtaking; for there remained at large, besides Howe, of the original gang who ran from the Derwent, only Septon, Jones, and Collier. — Coine and Browne, who were implicated in their recent robberies, were runaways from Fort Dalrymple.

In a few days after the affair in which Geary was killed, the banditti robbed several stock-keepers at the Carleton.

On the 3d of August, the little force of Serjeant McCarthy, which had been unremittingly scouring the woods in all directions, observed the print of feet on the beach, and traced and discovered the banditti at Swan Port, on the eastern shore.

As soon as they perceived the soldiers, they fled with precipitancy. One of the party fired, and shot Jones, their chief, through the head; who instantly died. His body was buried on the beach, after being decapitated, and his head sent to Hobart Town.

Whilst the party proceeded to intercept the retreat of the remainder, the fire of the banditti wounded Holmes (a runaway who had lately joined them), and he was taken; but from the intricacy of the woods, and his wounded state, he was with difficulty brought to Hobart Town.

We next find discontent and treachery among themselves hasten the destruction of the remainder of the banditti, for on the 25th of August, a horrible transaction occurred at a hut behind Gordon's Plains, near Launceston;

They had on that day effected a robbery at the farm of Mr Brumby, in which it appears Wright and Hillier, runaways from George Town, had joined them. On that evening Wright left the rest, and gave himself up at Launceston; but Hillier conceived the horrible project of murdering his companions, Septon and Collier, while asleep at this hut (it appears Coine and Browne were absent at this moment); imagining, as he afterwards laid, that he should receive the rewards offered by Government, and screen himself from the punishment of his own crimes, which he apprehended would speedily overtake him.

In the middle of the night, this monster, watching his opportunity, with a razor cut the throat of Septon from ear to ear, causing his immediate death ; he then turned to perpetrate the same act on Collier, who, it seems, had been slightly disturbed; he effected only a trifling wound on the neck of the latter, who made his escape out of the hut; Hillier, however, having previously secured possession of the arms, seized Septon's rifle gun, and fired at Collier, shattering his hand severely.

A more treacherous assassination has seldom been heard of.

Hillier was soon after taken; as was also Collier, in an enfeebled and helpless state. The former was sent to Sydney to take his trial for the murder of Septon, in the ship Pilot with Collier, who was sent to the fame tribunal, charged as one of the eight engaged in the murders at New Norfolk, when Carlisle and O'Birne were killed; and he was the only one reserved to make a public expiation.

Upon intelligence of this last dreadful affair, the Lieutenant Governor issued a further Proclamation, and offered the following rewards for the only three bush-rangers at large on the

1st day of September; viz.—

For Howe .... One hundred guineas;

Watts .... Eighty guineas;

Browne ..... Fifty guineas;

    All of whom were known to have no connexion or communication with each other.

## Proclamation,

By WILLIAM SORELL, *Esquire, Lieutenant Governor of Van Diemen's Land, &c. &c. &c.*

WHEREAS since the publication of a Proclamation, dated the 5th of July last, declaring Certain Rewards for the apprehension of the Bush-rangers, the greater part of the Banditti have been taken or destroyed, there remaining now at large GEORGE WATTS, charged with various Crimes and Robberies, BROWNE, a Frenchman, and MICHAEL HOWE, who recently absented himself after receiving an assurance of Clemency: And whereas the said MICHAEL HOWE stands charged with Murder and various Robberies; the following Rewards are proclaimed for the apprehension of the above Criminals :—

FOR MICHAEL HOWE, One Hundred Guineas ;

———GEORGE WATTS, Eighty - - - Ditto;

——— ——— BROWNE, Fifty - - - - Ditto.

Given under my Hand, at Government House, Hobart Town, this Sixth Day of September, 1817.

"WILLIAM SORELL."

By Command of His Honor the Lieutenant Governor,

    In this month Browne surrendered to Government; Coine and Keegan had done so some time previously ; and though capital punishment might have been inflicted on these last three, yet as they had no connexion with the heinous murders committed by others of the banditti, Government forbore to bring them before a Criminal Court. These men were chiefly companions of Parker, who was taken as before noticed, and with him were convicted by a Bench of Magistrates of various robberies, and sentenced—

Browne . . . 150 lashes, and 4 years to Newcastle;
Parker...
Coine . .. > 100 lashes each, and 2 years to ditto;
Keegan ...

We have now only Howe and Watts at large; and it seemed ordained that the greater should be reserved for punishment of the lesser villain, before called upon to receive the just reward of his great and manifold crimes.

On the 10th of October, Howe again appears on the scene, adding to the catalogue of murders already recorded one of the most savage character, which will long be in the recollection of the inhabitants of the Colony.

A person named William Drewe, alias Slambow, had charge of some sheep in the vicinity of New Norfolk, for his master, Mr. Williams of Hobart Town. Drewe had occasionally corresponded with Howe, and had agreed along with his master to take him on the first opportunity.

Howe had lately been at Williams's hut with a letter for the Lieutenant Governor; and soon after Watts, who it should seem had some design upon Howe, called to inquire of Drewe if he had seen him. Drewe informed Watts that he had seen Howe, and was to meet him at sun-rise the following Friday, when, he said, if Watts would come, he would take him. On the Thursday Watts took away a boat from New Norfolk in which he crossed the Derwent, and concealed himself near the path where Drewe had appointed, till the next morning. At sun-rise Drewe arrived, and told Watts that he was to meet Howe at a place called Long Bottom. They proceeded thither, and Watts requested Drewe to conceal his gun, as probably Howe would not come up to them if he perceived it. Upon arriving at the spot, Drewe called several times, and was answered by Howe from the opposite side of the creek. When Watts came within 90 yards of

Howe, he desired him to knock out the priming of his gun, promising to do the same; this was accordingly done by both, and after proceeding 30 or 40 yards, they made a fire. Soon after which, Watts caught hold of Howe, and threw him down; Drewe tied his hands, and took from his pockets two knives. Watts and Drewe next prepared breakfast, but of which Howe refused to partake. Before they proceeded to Hobart Town, Drewe proposed to take his master's gun and dog to the hut; which was agreed to by Watts, who desired him not to mention the occurrence of the morning to Williams; the latter had arrived the evening before at the hut to shear his sheep. Drewe met his master, who becoming, by the absence of his man, alarmed for his safety, had proceeded in search of him; upon Drewe's running towards him with his gun and dog, Williams inquired the cause; Drewe replied that George Watts was stopping with Howe, whom they had taken, whilst he came to acquaint his master, and deliver his musket, as he had got Michael Howe's, and Watts had his own; he also shewed Williams the two knives he had taken, but declined the offered assistance of the latter, as Howe was secured. Upon Drewe's return to Watts and Howe, they all proceeded towards Hobart Town; Watts with his gun loaded, walking before Howe, and Drewe behind. After walking about 8 miles, Howe found means to disengage his hands, and in an instant stabbed Watts, with a knife which he had remaining secreted about his person. Watts fell and dropped his gun, which Howe seized at the moment, and with it shot Drewe dead. Watts now dreaded a similar fate; for on asking Howe if he had killed Slambow, he replied "yes, and I'll serve you the same as soon as I can load the piece." Watts then ran about 200 yards, and lay down amongst some brush, being faint and cold from loss of blood. As soon as he was able to walk, he contrived to reach a settler's house not far distant, and, after being put to bed, told the owner that he had been stabbed by Howe, requesting the district constable might be sent for, to take him to town. Upon the arrival of the latter, Watts could only utter his own name; but the next morning he told the constable that

Drewe was killed. The body was found about half a mile from the house where Watts lay, and was conveyed to Hobart Town for a Coroner's Inquest, whose verdict was "That the deceased William Drewe was murdered by Michael Howe."

Watts was conveyed to gaol in a weakly state : he was a runaway from Newcastle, and was sent to Sydney in the Pilot, but under no criminal charge, where he died in the General Hospital, of the wounds received from Howe, in three days after his arrival.

As soon as the melancholy circumstance of the murder of Drewe was communicated to the Lieutenant Governor, he issued another Proclamation, promising, in addition to the former reward of 100 guineas, for the apprehension of Howe, a strong recommendation for a free pardon and passage to England, to any crown prisoner who would be the means of apprehending that great murderer, He was, however, not again seen for some time.

On the 25th of October, Collier was tried before the Criminal Court at Sydney, and convicted on the clearest evidence of being one of the murderers of Carlisle and O'Birne: he received sentence of death, to be executed at Hobart Town, and his body to be dissected. In December he was sent back to this Settlement; and suffered the sentence of the Law on the 26th of January, 1818. From the moment of this man's being taken, he professed to entertain no hope of mercy, but to prefer death, to the life he had lately led: he died penitent.

The once formidable gang, and the system of bush-ranging as an armed banditti, producing in it a progress great terror and mischief to the community, checking the views and paralysing the efforts of the settlers of this infant Colony, might now be considered annihilated; for, though Howe, the most hardened and sanguinary of the whole, still remained to be taken, yet he was cut off from association with man.

After the murder of Drewe, he was supposed to have buried himself in unknown and inaccessible parts of the woods: the necessity of procuring ammunition and supplies to prolong his wretched existence, compelled, however, his occasional appearance; and these supplies he obtained by robbing distant stock-keepers' huts; when he generally bore away with him as much as he could carry, threatening instant destruction to any person who would attempt to follow him, or trace his steps.

But his race was nearly run; and, though after the murder of Drewe and Watts, few would choose to risk a personal encounter with him, yet the confidence was pretty general that he could not long exist under his present circumstances.

One or two fruitless attempts were made to take him by stratagem. In the month of September, however, James McGill, who was the previous year emancipated for services against the bush-rangers with the 46th regiment, and who at different periods continued an assiduous pursuit after him, came so closely upon him that, in his hurry to escape, Howe left behind him his arms, ammunition, dogs, and knapsack, which fell into the hands of McGill, and were brought to Hobart Town.

The loss of his pistols on this occasion was a serious and irreparable one to Howe.

In his knapsack was found a sort of journal of dreams; which shew strongly the distressed state of his mind, and some tincture of superstition.

From this little book of kangaroo skin, written in kangaroo blood, it appears that he frequently dreamt of being murdered by natives, of seeing his old companions, Whitehead, Jones, Geary, and Collier, of being nearly taken by a soldier; and, in one instance, humanity asserts itself even in the breast of Michael Howe, for we find him recording that he dreamt of his sister.

It also appears from this memorandum book, that he had always an idea of settling in the woods; for it contains long, lists of such seeds as he wished to have, of vegetables, fruits and even flowers!

After this period, but one or two trifling robberies are heard of, in one of which he furnished himself with a gun, and anxiously inquired for pistols, before we come to the closing scene of the career of this desperado.

In the month of October, a person named Warburton, in the habit of hunting kangaroo for skins, who had occasional opportunities of seeing Howe, communicated to a crown prisoner, named Thomas Worrall, stock-keeper to Edward Lord, Esq. a scheme for taking him. Worrall agreed to the trial, and with private William Pugh, of the 48th regiment, a man of known courage, and recommended by Major Bell for this service, determined to lay in wait at a hut on the Shannon River, likely to be visited by Howe for supplies. Warburton was to look out for the approach of Howe, and to induce him to come to the hut, under a promise of ammunition; at the same time to signify his approach by a whistle.— This plan proved successful. On the 21st of October, Howe met Warburton near the place already mentioned; he, however, exhibited much distrust of the intention of the latter, and great hesitation in advancing near the hut, — often disappearing to see if any one were watching him. At length, after three hours indeterminate consideration, allured by promises of ammunition, which Warburton said was in the hut, be ventured to enter the door, his musket cocked and levelled; when Pugh instantly fired, but missed him. Howe simply exclaimed "Is that your game," and precipitately retreated, but at the same lime fired and missed also. Pugh and Worrall immediately rushed out to run him down, and the latter fired, but none of the shots took effect. Pugh and Worrall gained upon Howe; and now he must for once have felt appalled,— deprived of his pistols shortly before, no time allowed for a second charge, and his pursuers gaining ground, nothing but a miracle could effect his deliverance.— Pugh and Worrall had now come up with him; A severe encounter ensued; and finally, from well-directed blows on his head with their muskets, fell and expired without speaking the last of a lawless, murderous banditti! — exhibiting in his career and end the strongest proof of slow but certain retributive justice; which, though it was baffled for a season, in the end overwhelmed this wretched violator of its most sacred Laws with more striking vengeance ; after making him directly or indirectly the instrument of destruction to those connected with him in his dreadful outrages, he himself closed the scene! — an awful example which cannot be too strongly impressed upon the minds of all those who are inclined to prefer to the wholesome and mild Laws of civilized society, a licentious life of unrestraint; which can only be maintained by robbery and violence, and which will surely end in murder and ignominious death!

Howe was of athletic make: he wore at the time of his death a dress made of kangaroo skins; had an extraordinary long beard, and presented altogether a terrific appearance. His face, perhaps in some degree from associating with it the recollection of his crimes, exhibited strong marks of a murderer. During his long career of guilt, he was never known to perform one humane act: His body was interred on the spot where he fell; his head was brought to Hobart Town, and suffered to be seen by the people, to whom the end of this monster afforded an inconceivable degree of satisfaction.

The reward due to the zeal and bravery of the persons engaged in ridding the world of this murderer was universally acknowledged to be well merited. His Honor Lieutenant Governor Sorell issued a Government and General Order, in which he strongly commended the activity, intelligence, and spirit of private William Pugh, whom His Honor recommends to His Excellency the Governor in Chief for the greatest favour he can receive. The deserving conduct of Thomas Worrall His Honor also brings under the notice of His Excellency, accompanied by a strong recommendation for a free pardon and passage to England, in pursuance of the terms of the Proclamation.

The reward for Howe's apprehension was adjudged to be divided in the following manner: —

To Pugh £50; to Worrall £40, and to Warburton (who was not personally engaged) £15.

THE following account of the unhappy end of Edward Edwards and John Bowles, and the sudden disappearance of Thomas Davenport, all crown servants, as connected with Howe's crimes, and adding to the number of those who fell by his murderous hand, proceed from the fame authority :

After the banditti, in an early stage, had taken a Government boat from Port Dalrymple, they robbed Captain Townson of a cask of pork, and went to King's Island, where they hid a box of tools in the sand: they next went to Cape Barren, where they disagreed and separated. A further dispute arose, when Howe, it is stated, deliberately shot Edwards, in the presence of Jones and Whitehead.

On a subsequent occasion, at a creek on Salt-pan Plains, Bowles having sportively discharged a pistol over Howe's head, the latter in a wanton and cruel manner tied Bowles, hand and feet, and then coolly shot him dead.

Thomas Davenport, who was an aligned servant to Mr. D. Stanfield, obtained his master's permission to hunt kangaroo in the interior of the country; taking with him a musket, dogs, and other necessaries. He had not been absent more than three days, when his dogs returned without him.—This circumstance created much anxiety, which was Increased by Davenport not being heard of, and all inquiry alter him proving unavailing, for some time. At length Warburton (mentioned in the foregoing narrative), in a conversation with Howe, was told by him that Davenport was killed by the natives. The general belief, however, is that Howe had met Davenport, and in some way been the cause of his death; — perhaps sacrificed him on a refusal to join in his enormities.

The public have thus a brief narrative of the chief events of the last six years of Howe's life; comprising a series of crimes committed with the coolest indifference. Many committed previously to the surrender of the gang, and others of less enormity, have been omitted; and most of the information given by himself disregarded as proceeding from such a man.

The bush-rangers had no fixed place of general rendezvous, or any regular system;— they were, of necessity, constantly moving about the woods; frequently without the common support and necessaries of life, and exposed to much hardship. They could never have become formidable, had not the peculiar circumstances of the Colony admitted of their becoming better acquainted with the interior than other men; and it is nearly impossible that any bands of future bush-rangers will be formed, or, if formed, that they can exist for long unsubdued as those now happily exterminated.

Hobart, December 1818.

Popular dramatist John H. Amherst used Wells book to create the first play about Tasmania. It premiered at London's Royal Coburg Theatre in April 1821, and was revived in October 1821 as an actor's benefit.

LOST, about a Month ago, off the Road from the Cove-hill towards the Half-way-hill, by a Person proceeding to Port Dalrymple on horseback, a Parcel which was fastened to the crupper, containing the following articles; viz.—A yellow spotted marcella Waistcoat, a pair of grey-cloth Trowsers, two Shirts, two pair of Stockings, and 13 Pamphlets of Michael Howe the late Bush-ranger, which were tied up very close in two Handkerchiefs, one silk, the other cotton.—Whoever has found the same and will bring them to the Printer of this Paper will receive Two Pounds Reward; and if after this Public Notice they should be found in the Possession of any Person, the Parties will be prosecuted.

Andrew Bent's notice in April 1819 regarding the loss of 13 copies.

ART. II.—*Michael Howe, the last and worst of the Bush Rangers of Van Diemen's Land. Narrative of the Chief Atrocities committed by this Great Murderer and his Associates, during a Period of Six Years, in Van Diemen's Land. From authentic sources of information.* Hobart Town. Printed by Andrew Bent. 12mo. 1818.

THIS is the greatest literary curiosity that has yet come before us—the first child of the press of a state only fifteen years old ! It will of course be reprinted here;—but our copy, the copy *penes nos*, is a genuine Caxton, *rarissimus*—nay more, it hath the title-page. Few impressions were thrown off at the Hobart Town Press, for the settlement does not greatly abound in readers; and we therefore recommend the Roxburghe Club to apply early for a copy, for this little book will assuredly be the ' Reynarde the Foxe' of Australian bibliomaniacs.

Review of *Michael Howe* in the London ⊠ *uarterly Review* 1820.

# MATTHEW BRADY

## INTRODUCTION

In December, 1821, Lieutenant-Governor William Sorell selected Macquarie Harbour, an inlet of the sea on the western coast of Tasmania, about 200 miles by water from Hobart, as a place of punishment for the worst class of criminals. So dreary was the region, so harsh the conditions of life, and so ferocious the punishments inflicted, that during the first five years of its establishment at least half of the two hundred prisoners confined there attempted to escape. Some perished; some were retaken; others formed bushranging gangs, the most notorious of which was that led by Matthew Brady, an educated man, who had been transported to New South Wales and there sent to Van Diemen's Land for gross insubordination.

The narrative of his career begins early in June 1824, when Lieutenant-Governor Sir George Arthur was in command of the Tasmanian settlement. Brady, at that time a confinee at Macquarie Harbour, with twelve fellow convicts, attempted to seize a boat belonging to Wright, the Commandant there , who, however, managing to get it into the water, shoved off before they could capture it, though he was compelled to leave behind him the gaol surgeon, whom the gang made preparations to flog. But Brady, who when a patient in the hospital had experienced some kindnesses from the surgeon, interposed and saved him from the triangle.

The gang next seized another boat owned by some of the soldiers, in which, nine days later, on the 18th, they arrived at the outskirts of Hobart. There they visited the home of a certain Mr. Mason, whom they treated with great violence and cruelty. Some few days afterwards they appeared at Clarence Plains, where they held up and robbed Mr. Patrick Brodie. When, however, they attacked and deprived

Sir George Arthur.

of his firearms a servant of Lieutenant Gunn, the latter pursued and captured five of them, who were tried at once and executed, along with Alexander Pearce, the man-eater.[1] During the next two years Brady and his gang systematically raided the settlements from Launceston to Sorell, distinguishing themselves by their daring and activity.

Very shortly after their escape, Governor Arthur issued the first of his proclamations:-

"The Lieutenant-Governor feels it necessary to announce that the party of prisoners who escaped from Macquarie Harbour, have again passed into the interior. His Honor begs in the most earnest manner to call upon all settlers in their respective districts to enter with increased zeal and determination into measures for the apprehension of these robbers. To the most common understanding, not labouring under the most miserable depression of personal danger, means will be presented, after a robbery has been committed, of tracing the movements of the depredators; and it must be understood to be the positive duty of any settler to spread the information immediately, and to adopt the most prompt and energetic steps for closely pursuing these miscreants until they are fairly hunted down. All Crown servants are to be assembled immediately by their masters, and apprized that the Government expects that every man shall give all possible information that may lead to the apprehension of these bushrangers."

Many exciting incidents in connexion with the career of Brady and his satellites are on record. On one occasion, for example, a Mr. Kemp was accosted by Brady and his party, and taken to his master's house, where he was ordered to gain admission, which he did by answering his employer's challenge. The bushrangers then entered, took possession of the place and ransacked it, even though seven assigned servants and two free labourers were present. On another occasion, near Oatland, a young lad acting as cook to a party of soldiers met Brady and his desperadoes. Himself anxious to join the robber band, he led the bushrangers up to the houses of the soldiers, whom they covered with their loaded muskets. They then tied them up, robbed them of all their valuables and departed, taking the lad with them. Growing bolder with success, they attacked a squatter's home, demanded free quarters from the overseer, were well treated by the convict servants, who had some measure of sympathetic affinity with them, carried off everything of value, and ended up by burning the farmer's accumulated store of wool.

The settlers most exposed to attack, West tells us, "often abandoned the business of their farms; their buildings were perforated with loopholes, their men were posted as sentinels, and all the preparations necessary to a state of war were adopted."[2]  Finding that a reward of £10 per head offered for the apprehension of the offenders was entirely in adequate, Governor Arthur, stirred to action by the complaints of the settlers, issued his second Government Proclamation:-

Government House,
April 14th, 1825.

It has occasioned the Lieutenant-Governor much concern that the continued outrages of the two convicts, McCabe[3] and Brady, have led to the death of another settler, His Honor has directed that a reward of £25 shall be given for the apprehension of either of these men; and that any prisoner apprehending and securing either of them, in addition to the above reward, shall receive a conditional pardon. The magistrates are very pressingly desired to circulate this order, and to direct the constables to visit all huts of stock-keepers, shepherds, and others in their respective districts, notifying the rewards offered, and cautioning such persons against receiving, harbouring, or supporting these men, who are charged with the commission of murder. Fifty acres of land, free from restrictions, will be given to the Chief Constable in whose district either McCabe or Brady is taken, provided it shall be certified by the magistrate of the district that he has zealously exerted himself in the promulgation of this order, and to the adoption of measures for giving it effect.

The magistrates will see the importance of conveying timely information of the movements of McCabe and Brady; and will consider

Matthew Brady.

themselves duly authorised to incur any responsible expenses in so doing.

By command of His Honor, the Lieutenant-Governor,

JOHN MONTAGU, Secretary

Brady's reply was an impudent notice, posted on the door of the Royal Oak Inn at Crossmarch:-

Mountain Home,

April 20th, 1828.

"It has caused Matthew Brady much concern that such a person known as Sir George Arthur is at large. Twenty gallons of rum will be given to any person that will deliver his person unto me. I also caution John Priest that I will hang him for his ill-treatment of Mrs. Blackwell, at Newtown."

One of Brady's most daring exploits was the taking of the town of Sorell, the capture of the gaol, and the release of the prisoners. Eight in number, the bushrangers made a quick descent on the town of Pittwater, where they began a general plunder. Entering the premises of Mr. Walter Bethune, who was temporarily absent, they took possession, imprisoned the servants, and remained there roystering for a couple of days. When, on the following day, Mr. Bethune and a Colonel Bunster arrived, they also were caught and detained. It is related that they stripped these two victims of their clothing, offering their own in exchange. As Bunster would not agree, he was reduced to spending the night wrapped in a single blanket. Then, at about ten o'clock in the evening, with eighteen prisoners, including Bethune and Bunster, all securely tied up, the gang set out for Sorell.

Within the gaol, a party of soldiers, who had been out in the rain all day in pursuit of the malefactors, was engaged cleaning their muskets. Taken entirely by surprise, they were easily captured and locked up, with the eighteen others, in the cells from which the inmates were removed. To the latter Brady offered their liberty, which was accepted by all but one, a man charged with a capital offence for which he was afterwards hanged. The gaolor, who had managed to escape, ran and informed the surgeon and the Commanding officer, Lieutenant Gunn.

When the former came on the scene, he too was caught and shut up with the others. When Gunn arrived, he was shot so severely in the arm that it proved necessary to amputate the limb.[4] The outlaws, having propped up the gaol door with a log dressed to look like a sentry, then escaped.

Many stories are told of the atrocities committed by the Brady gang. Lieutenant Breton vouches for the authenticity of the following:[5]

A man by whom he (Brady) had frequently been harboured, at length determined to betray him, so as to be entitled to the reward offered for his capture, and for this purpose concealed two constables in his hut.

When Brady was about to approach the hut, where he had been so often before, suspicion arose in his mind that all was not right. On observing this to a man who was with him, the latter said it was highly improbable that the owner of the hut would betray him, after all that had passed between them. Without being the least convinced of the soundness of the argument, he advanced, and when near enough was fired upon by the constables. The result was a wound in the arm, and the seizure of himself and his companion; the latter was marched off, in charge of the constables, to the nearest magistrate, and Brady was left bound under the charge of his betrayer. After a while the former asked his quondam friend to let him lie on the bed, and to place over him a kangaroo rug, as his wound was very painful. His request being complied with, he availed himself of the opportunity to extricate his hands from the cord by which they were bound, and then asked for water. While procuring same, the man laid aside his gun, which being perceived by Brady, he sprang from the bed and laid hold of it, so as completely to turn the tables upon his treacherous keeper.

When a prisoner, Brady had reproached him for having acted with such perfidy to one who had placed implicit confidence in him, he only replied by observing that Brady could but be hanged, which was of no consequence, as there was neither God or devil! As soon, however, as he found himself in the power of the man whom he had injured, and that he might dread the worst from his vengeance, the craven threw himself on his knees, and in the most abject manner begged, for God's sake, that his life might be spared! Brady replied, "You are a pretty rascal to use the name of God, after having told me there was none. However, I will not shoot you now, as an alarm might be created by the report of my gun, but if we meet again!" Brady then made his escape.

Afterwards, when commanding a regular gang of bushrangers, he fell in with this same man, seized him, and, holding a pistol to his head, told him he had just five minutes left to say his prayers. When he perceived his death resolved upon, he coolly placed his head again at the door of a hut by which they were standing, and said, "Then fire, and be damned to you!" upon which he was shot dead. When the body was discovered, the bullet was found to have barely penetrated the skull, and was quite flattened.

The whole of Tasmania now became profoundly alarmed, for travelling had become dangerous, the bushrangers perpetrating numerous acts not only of wanton destruction, but also of cruelty. One of their favourite pleasantries, according to West, was to force people of an establishment to drink so much liquor that they were incapable of following him.

With the wanton burning of Mr. Elliott's property came another wave of excitement and indignation. The whole country was up in arms against the bushrangers, who were sought in every quarter. Permission having been given for prisoners to unite with the bushrangers in order to betray them, men wearing irons, as though they had just escaped from custody, but who were keen to secure not only the Governor's rewards but also their own pardons, left Hobart secretly, joined the robbers, and then gave, or attempted to give, information to the police. Brady and his crew, however, soon grew wise to this device and visited their wrath on any suspected or would-be informers.

As a result of the Governor's vigorous measures, several conflicts took place between the bandits and their prisoners, both of whom were well armed. In less than a month after the second proclamation, many of the offenders were safely in gaol. So intense was the feeling in the Colony at this time that there is on record the presentation of a petition to Governor Arthur, signed by fifty prominent citizens, praying that the prisoners under arrest might be speedily executed, in order that all fear of their escape from gaol might be removed from the public mind.[6]

Commenting on this petition, the Chief Justice remarked: "It is common for private individuals to deprecate the severities of public justice, but the awful state of the Colony must be admitted, when fifty persons among its most opulent and ever humane inhabitants were anxious to hasten the offices of the executioner."

According to the *Hobart Town Gazette* for 1825, "not less than one hundred men were in arms at that time; most of them were absconders from the various penal stations, and had exhausted all those forms of severity which stopped short of the scaffold," while West asserts that during the two years ending with 1826, one hundred and three persons suffered death, and that at one sitting of the Court, thirty-seven were sentenced to death, of whom, twenty-three were executed in the course of a fortnight, nine suffering together and fourteen others in two days closely following.

In a spirit of exasperation, Arthur issued his Third Proclamation, five hundred copies of which were scattered throughout the Colony. In this he threatened with death any person found harbouring an offender. The rewards were largely increased; for every named bushranger, one hundred guineas or three hundred acres of land; or to prisoner; money and a free pardon; to the chief constable in whose district a robber should be captured, one hundred acres. Arthur complained, too, that sufficient energy and co-operation had not been employed, and called upon the magistrates and other loyal citizens to free the Colony of the menace. He himself changed his residence to Jericho, so that he could personally direct operations. The people of Hobart formed themselves into a civic guard, so that the regular constables might be released for this special service. Soldiers, hidden in drays, were driven along the roads with the hope of coming upon Brady or some members of his gang. It was probably about this date that *The Van Diemen's Land Warriors* of which the full text is printed in this volume, was written though, for some unexplained reason, it was not published till 1827.

Appearing suddenly in the suburbs of Launceston, Brady next sent word to the Commandant there, "with the bushrangers' compliments," that he proposed to rob the house of a Mr. Dry, and on the same night to attack the gaol, carry off a prisoner named Jeffries confined then; and put him to death. This message, though treated with contempt and even jocularity, proved to be no idle threat, for the bushrangers, landing from a vessel they had seized, advanced upon the home of Mr. Dry, who was entertaining a party of friends. Having plundered the place, they were packing up their booty when Colonel Balfour, who had been summoned, arrived with ten soldiers and surrounded the house. The robbers then retreated to the back part of the premises and fired into the rooms. When at dark, the firing having ceased, it was thought that they had departed, the Colonel, with four of his men, hastened away to protect the town, to which Brady had despatched part of his band. As soon as he had gone some of the bandits again showed themselves, and hostilities were resumed. When Dr. Priest, the surgeon, and Mr. Theodore Bartley joined forces with the soldiers, the former had his horse shot dead under him, and was himself wounded in the knee, an injury from the effects of which he died. Again the gang escaped capture.

Still at large, Brady did not lack followers, for many desperate escaped convicts rallied round him. Ross's *Van Diemen's Land Annual* for 1833 contains a succinct account of some of the atrocities committed in 1826:

On the night of the 5th, the bushrangers set fire to and burnt down the stockyard with all the wheat belonging to Mr. Abraham Walker and Commissary Walkeropposite. Mr. Thomas Archer's : The extent of the damage is not yet ascertained. The bushrangers were seen between the punt and Mr. Gibson's stockyard, and on the 6th they sent word to Mr. Massey, on the South Esk, Ben Lamond, that they would

John Batman, who arrested Matthew Brady.

hang him and burn his wheat. A great fire was seen in the direction of his house, but it is to be hoped that they have not executed their threat. The bushrangers have Mr. Dry's two white carriage horses with them. They shot Thomas Kenton dead at the punt on the South Esk; they called him out of his house and deliberately shot him. Two runaways were last week sent into Launceston from Pressnell's, where they were taken. One of them broke out of gaol, and was met by the bushrangers, who asked him to join them, and, on his refusal, they shot him dead.

Brady now wears Colonel Balfour's cap, which was knocked off at Dry's. When the bushrangers were going down the Tamar they captured Captain White, of the Duke of York in his boat; Captain Smith, late of the Brutus, who was with him, being mistaken for Colonel Balfour, they knocked him down, but, discovering their mistake, they apologised. They then made Captain White go down on his knees, and were going to shoot him, but Captain Smith interfered and saved his life, on representing to them the misery it would inflict on his children. During the night Captains Smith and White were allowed to depart, and they made the best of their way to Launceston, where they gave the necessary information; but unfortunately it was too late, the bushrangers having crossed the river .

Still Brady evaded capture, though one by one his companions were rounded up. Once he was wounded in the ankle, but managed to get away. At last, early in 1826, John Batman, famous for the part he played in the Black War and in the settlement of Port Phillip, succeeded in running him down amongst the gullies of the Western Tiers. Unkempt and dejected, he was apparently still suffering great pain from his injury, and on being surprised, surrendered to Batman when he learned that he was not a soldier, for he held the military in supreme contempt and abhorrence. He was taken to Hobart Town, where he was confined in the gaol with the notorious Jeffries, with whom he firmly refused to associate. Trial, conviction and the death sentence followed in quick succession. James Bonwick, the historian, tells us the aftermath of the trial. He says:-

Petition followed petition for his deliverance from the halter. Settlers told of his forbearance, and ladies of his kindness. His cell was besieged with visitors, and his table was loaded with presents. Baskets of fruits, bouquets of flowers and dishes of confectionery prepared by his fair admirers, were tendered in abundance to the gaoler for his distinguished captive. The last moment came. The dramatic scene was maintained to its close. Pinioned, he stood on the scaffold before a dense mass of spectators, who cheered him for his courage, or grieved bitterly for his fate. He received the consolations of the, Roman Catholic faith, he bade a familiar adieu to the gentlemen about him, and he died more like a patient martyr than a felon murderer.

In the *Sydney Gazette* of 24th May 1826, will be found an account of the execution of Brady and his gang, copied from the Tasmanian journals. These executions took place on two successive days — Brady, Jeffries, Perry, Thompson and Bryant on one day, and the whole of the remainder on the following day. The Rev. William Bedford, Senior Anglican Chaplain, administered consolation to the Protestants, and the Rev. Father Philip Connolly to the Roman Catholics.

Romance and chivalry are still moving elements in human make-up, so that the sympathy extended to Brady, and to many criminals of his ilk, is quite a common phenomenon. In Brady's case there may have been some reason for his popularity, for, Robin Hood-like, he boasted that he never killed a man intentionally, that he ever treated women with respect and courtesy, and that he severely punished members of his gang who violated these principles of conduct. On the whole, Brady seems to have been one of the least inhuman of the Tasmanian bushrangers.

# The Van Diemen's Land Warriors

In the British Museum, bound up with a number of pamphlets relating to Tasmania and collected by Thomas Scott, of Earlston, is one of the only four copies known of a verse satire connected with the hunt for Matthew Brady and his gang. It is entitled *The Van Diemen's Land Warriors, or The Heroes of Cornwall,* by Pindar JuvenaL    The second copy is in the Petherick Collection of the National Library, Canberra, the third in the Mitchell Library, Sydney, and the fourth in the possession of a Tasmanian collector.  The date of publication is 1827, and the printer the famous Andrew Bent, of Hobart Town. Historically, the greatest interest attaching to "The Warriors" lies in the fact that it is the very first volume of verse printed in Tasmania. Here, in brief, is the story of the satire:-

In Canto One, a Baker, a Cobbler, a Tailor, a Black- smith, a Carpenter, a Grocer's Apprentice, a Pastrycook and a Hatter resolve - in long speeches full of very cheap italicised puns - to join in hunting down the dreaded bushranger, Matthew Brady. A Parson's Clerk gives them his blessing, but prefers to stay at home in Launceston.

In Canto Two, they discuss the leadership of the expedition, and eventually choose the tailor, apparently, because, like the pedlar in the Interlude of "The 4 P's," he is the greatest liar. Under him they march off, to find, after a short walk, that he has forgotten to bring any bullets, and has supplied them with lampblack instead of gunpowder. These deficiencies having been remedied, they start off again, and in the dusk of the evening suddenly happen upon Brady and his gang, all asleep and snoring loudly. With one accord they run away, Captain Snip, the tailor, in the lead still.

Canto Three tells how, after recovering their spirits, they retrace their steps, rediscover the gang, and open fire. Every man misses, but the noise of the volley awakens the sleepers, who turn out to be a herd of donkeys. The noise has also awakened two soldiers of the 40th Regiment, who are out after Brady. Rushing to the spot, these arrest as bushrangers the thirteen valiant Bobadils — how their numbers continued to grow from the original nine to thirteen Pindar Juvenal does not attempt to explain. The soldiers take them to the nearest magistrate, who releases them with some caustic comments. The next day they actually do happen on Brady, who marches them off to his strong- hold, threatens to kill them, and in the end compromise; by giving them fifty lashes each, with a double allowance for Captain Snip. They are then deprived of their trousers and made to walk back into Launceston thus stripped.

As far as can be ascertained, the whole story is fictitious, for it cannot be fitted into any known incident or series of incidents in Brady's career. Publication of the volume was announced in the *Colonial Times* on 6th October, 1827, and in *The Australian* of 7th November, more than a year after the execution of Brady. For this delay in publication no reason can now be discovered.

Of the four extant copies, two are particularly important bibliographically. That in the National Library, Canberra, of which the title-page is reproduced herein, bears in the margin the signature, in pen writing, of J. A. Thomson. A pencil note in this copy, however, which states that the author, "Pindar Juvenal," was James Atkinson, is obviously a misreading and misidentification of Thomson for Atkinson, a careful examination of the signature will show.

In the Mitchell Library copy there is inscribed in ink of long years' standing, beneath the words "Pindar Juvenal," on the title-page, the Words "Robert Wales of Launceston." The evidence, therefore, is that he was the author. According to Morris Miller.[7] the Mitchell Library records reveal that in 1831 Robert Wales was appointed Registrar to the Court of Requests at Launceston. In Ross's *Hobart Town Almanack* for 1836, his name also appears as Summoning Officer at Launceston, with a salary of £150 per annum. The Mitchell Library also possesses a letter written by Wales in 1845, and another written to him in 1852, requesting him to raise funds for the Franklin search expedition. So much for Wales.

Inserted in the Canberra copy is a typewritten note, copied from an article by "Anobium" in *The Argus* of 18th February, 1911, entitled "Banned Books: Rare Australian Works." It reads:

"Without doubt, the most interesting of suppressed Australian books is a work called *Van Diemen's Land Warriors*. Besides having been suppressed, it has the merit of having been perhaps the first verse published in Van Diemen's Land. It bears the date 1827, and is a satire on the military forces for their repeated failures to put an end to the bushranging of those evil days. The common law of the times knew nothing of the punctilious technicalities which attach to legal proceedings nowadays. There was a vague feeling among the underlings of the law that this was a wicked book. They submitted it to a man named James Thomson, a schoolmaster. He does not seem to have been even a J.P., or to have any authority at all. But, perhaps to curry favour with the officials, he declared the book to be libellous and advised that every obtainable copy should be burned. This was done, but Thomson kept his own copy, which after many years of adventure, finally fell into the hands of Mr. E. A. Petherick, now the Commonwealth Librarian, who has it among the many wonderful treasures in his custody at Federal Parliament House. The value of this copy is not known, as this copy is probably unique" — which, of course, it is not, since three other copies have now been discovered.[8]

At the end of the First Canto in the National Library copy, is another note, presumably written by J. A. Thomson:

"The reader cannot but take notice of the libelous matter contained in the verses which are underlined. As likewise the undeserved and uncalled for slur upon the Military throughout the whole of the work. Surely men and officers who have seen the service they have and assisted to fight so many battles, cannot be justly called cowards.

"My opinion of this work is that it should be suppressed and every existing copy burnt."

J.A.T.

It is upon this note that "Anobium" apparently based his opinion that Thomson was called on to censor the work. His view that it was libellous and should be suppressed may have been only his own private note. There is no evidence that his opinion was brought to the notice of the authorities or that they acted upon his recommendation.

Concerning the identity of this J.A. Thomson, Morris Miller says: "There came to Hobart in 1823 a Scotch emigrant, named James Thomson, who owned a boarding school there during 1823-1838. He afterwards became a government official. In 1856 he removed to the Geelong District, Victoria, where his brother (?) Dr. Alexander Thomson, was a prominent figure. He died in 1859. James Thomson took an active part in local theological controversies and published some pamphlets. His work is recorded in J. Heyer's *The Presbyterian Pioneers of Van Diemen's Land* (1935). While this James Thomson may have been concerned in an unofficial suppression of *The Van Diemen's Land Warriors*, the signature in the Commonwealth Library's copy does not conform to his own initials. Another James Thomson, a convict, was recommended for pardon in a petition, dated August, 1832. In 1831 a Scotch architect, James Alexander Thomson (born 1805), arrived in Hobart and practised his profession. He died in 1860." Apart from this, history is silent.

The text of *The Van Diemen's Land Warriors*, of which a line-for-line and page-for-page reprint follows, is taken from the copy bearing the signature of J.A. Thomson in the Petherick collection of the National Library, Canberra, to which I desire to acknowledge my obligation. The passages underlined are those that he himself underlined. Such typographical errors as appear in the text are repeated from the original.

"PROBATION" STATION IN VAN DIEMEN'S LAND.

The View from Brady's Lookout, Rosevears, Tasmania.

# THE
## Van Diemen's Land Warriors,
### OR THE
# HEROES OF CORNWALL;

# SATIRE,
### IN
# Three Cantos.

## BY PINDAR JUVENAL.

"ARMA VIRUMQUE CANO."

---

## Tasmania:
### PRINTED BY ANDREW BENT,
#### COLONIAL TIMES OFFICE.

SOLD FOR THE AUTHOR, BY W. WYLDE, WELLINGTON
BRIDGE, ELIZABETH-STREET, HOBART TOWN;
AND JAMES ASH, BRISBANE-STREET,
LAUNCESTON.—PRICE, 3s.

1827

# Dedication.

---

To my best and most sincere friend — MYSELF.

Sir,

Severed as I am from my native Isle, far from my dearest relatives and friends, and dwelling in a country where genuine friendship is so rare, I cannot too highly appreciate that inestimable blessing, when smiling fortune throws it in my way. Convinced as I am that no one has my welfare more at heart than *yourself* — that in adversity you would feel my misfortunes as your *own* — that in my prosperity you would *sincerely rejoice* ; and feeling as I do, that you are almost the only friend in whom I can place *implicit confidence*, permit me, as a mark of my extreme regard and gratitude for friendship so truly sincere, to dedicate to you this offspring of my Muse, and to assure you how much

I am,
Sir,
Your obliged
Obedient servant,
Pindar Juvenal.

# CONTENTS

## OF THE

## First Canto.

—◆—

The meeting of the heroes to discuss the state of Van
Diemen's Land, and to devise means for capturing
the notorious gang of bush-rangers, headed by the
outlaw Brady. — The Baker's magnanimous speech
— his reflection on the prowess of the Military. —
The speech of the Cobbler, who threatens to leather the banditti. — The Tailor's gallant oration.
The Blacksmith's speech, in which he reflects upon
the soldiers for not having nailed the banditti long
before. — The Carpenter's speech — he inveighs
against the measures taken by Colonel Arthur for
capturing the bush-rangers — his contempt for the
soldiers. — The Barber's speech — his desire for taking Brady by the nose — his saving disposition.—
The valorous oration of the Grocer's Apprentice —
His opinion of the soldier's courage.—The tart reply
of the Pastry-cook. — The Tinker's speech. — The
Hatter's declamation. — The speech of the Parson's Clerk — his prudent resolve. — The Tailor's
indignation.

THE

# *Warriors of Van Diemen's Land,*

OR THE

## HEROES OF CORNWALL.

——◄•►——

# Canto First.

——◆——

War, and those gallant souls, I proudly chant,
Whose lion hearts did bravely fiercely pant—
To capture Brady, and his ruffian band,
Who reigned the terror of Van Diemen's Land ;
I sing the meeting of the valiant crew,
Who met to argue what was best to do,
What was the sure and most effectual plan,
To take the lives of Brady's murd'rous clan ;
Oh ! Wellington, the feats that I'll report,
Will make thy brav'ry dwindle into nought ;
The fields of Talavera—Waterloo—
Were nought, compared to what the muse will shew !

Now to my tale ; the muse shall be sincere,

And tell the speech of every volunteer,
Who met that day, with fierce and knowing face,
To argue soundly poor Van Diemen's case.
A *Baker* first got up and sagely said,
T'was hard that Settlers who came there for *bread*
Whose *bread* was *scarce enough* to keep themselves,
Should thus be plundered by a *batch* of elves,
Gem'men said he, those rogues *have done too much*
My blood now *rises*, and my thoughts are such,
The *soldiers* never will divest the land
Of this terrific, plund'ring, murd'rous band ;
The thought now *kindles* in my breast a *fire*
Of emulation, and a proud desire
To take the field with pistols, sword, and gun,
And kill the rascals, every mother's son,
Who for their *balm* and comfort will be shoven
With *peals* of thunder, into Satan's *oven*.

The Cobbler rose. and swore upon his *sole*,*
That with so brave a corps he would enrol ;
Said he, if *awl*† will *stick like wax together*,
Our *end* is gained, the scoundrels we shall *leather* :
And then for *awl*† their thefts and murders past,
That very day shall be the scoundrel's *last*,

* Soul.                                        † All

In Brady's *shoes* to stand, I would not do't,
For *awl* the Indies and the world to *boot* !

Fierce as that warlike animal called *mutton*,
The Tailor rose, and vowed that not a *button*
He cared for fighting Brady's lawless band,
Or any such disturbers of the land,
Who on the highway sculked in search of riches,
And *cabbaged* money from a trav'ler's *breeches* ;
Indeed, no man should rob him of a dollar !
The man who trid it he would quickly *collar*,
And give the fellow such a hearty dose,
In fact he'd shoot the villain like a *goose* !
He's quickly end the robber's highway strife,
And fearless *cut* the rascal's *thread* of life !
Then told his friends most modestly that he
Was sharp as a *needle* or a pin could be,
That if they really wished to shoot them,
*He* was the very fellow that would *suit them* !

Next was a *Blacksmith*, who aloud declaimed,
And said the soldiers could not but be blamed,
That had they not in martial duty failed,
Brady and all his gang had long been *nailed* ;
As Brady and all his gang are near this spot,
Let's *strike the blow* whilst yet the *iron's hot* !

To arms, let's go ! I know of nought that hinders
Our *blowing* all the rebel knaves to *cinders* ;
Whilst there's a *spark* of *fire* within my breast,
'Till they be killed these limbs shall never rest ;
Curs'd be the man that tries to *quench* the *flame*,
That cannot fail t'immortalize my name !
My *heat* of *temper*, pray excuse my friends,
When I begin, God knows where passion ends !
It is a *vice*, that with much truth is said,
Cannot be *knocked* too soon upon the *head* ;
For when it long in mortal's bosom reigns
It *steels* the heart against true friendship's *chains*.


Now spake a *Carpenter*, who vowed he *saw*
Quite *plane*,\* that nought could bring the rogues to
   law,
Unless the gem'man there *joined* hand in hand,
To *cut* in pieces Brady's daring band,
(Which to the country was a horrid *bore*,
And which he *augured* migh be killed before
The *compass* of a week or little more ;)
He wished to *axe*† the gentlemen if they
Did not with him most solemnly enveigh
Against the silly *rules* and *measures* planned

---

    \* Plain                             † Ask

By Colonel Arthur, Governor of the land,
Who sent out soldiers to destroy the band ?
Soldiers, indeed ! why he himself would fight
A dozen such, and put them *awl** to flight !
But as he always acted on the *square*,
He'd rather have the angry battle fair,
And fight *one* soldier, *if* one soldier dare ;
Come on, he cried ! let's take our warlike *tools*,
And *drive* the robbers from their lurking holes ;
If we go out to take the rebel mob
By Jove, my friends, we'll maken no *wooden job !*

Down sat the carpenter ; a *Barber* rose,
And hoped he'd soon have Brady by the *nose* ;
To fight against him no one could be prouder,
In fact, he'ad all his life been used to *powder* ;
Then by the *beard of Mahomet* he swore
He'd *comb* the *wigs* of Brady's gang before
Another week, he'd *trim* the rogues depraved,
Or else he hoped his soul might not be saved ;
Happy was he to say he did not care
For Brady's lawless troop a single *hair ;*
His gallant friends assembled there, God bless them,
He thought were just the boys to *strap* and *dress*
     them ;

---

* All.

And should they *all* the rebel villains shoot,
He'd make a charge, and *cut* each rascal's *throat* !
Then being bless'd with feelings rather saving,
He asked his friends if no one *wanted shaving*,
Which at that time was not *bienseant* behaving !

A *Grocer's dapper little 'prentice* next
Got up, and said he'd very oft' been vexed
To think the soldiers had not long ago
Captured both Brady and his hellish crew ;
As for *his* part, he did not care a *plum,*
If Brady's party should that minute come ;
The rogues he knew would not a minute stay,
His *muster'd* friends would *pepper* them away ;
They'd find, and find too late t'was wrong to pop
Their scoundrel heads into so wrong a *shop* ;
Come take your arms, my friends, I'm much in doubt
If Brady's party will be ta'en without !
A *fig* for soldiers, I alone would handle
A soldier as if he were a *farthing candle* !
Of soldier's courage some folks make such fuss,
Can they be put upon a *scale* with us ?
But *still*, if should our Gov'nor of the land
Invest in me th' absolute command
Of twelve stout soldiers, with their Captain too,
I'd undertake to make them beat the foe ;

For I conceive in war successful deeds,
Much, much depend upon the man who leads !

A *Pastry Cook* then made a *tart reply*,
And said it was his duty to deny,
That no King's soldier could be reckoned brave,
For he that very moment chanced to have
*High* in the army two most valiant boys,
Who in that army made *no little noise*,
As he had lately been informed by one,
Who'd been a witness to the deeds they'd done ;
Though in their praises he would fain be dumb,
Yet, braver fellows never *beat a drum !*
At other's cost he never wished to *puff*,
The merits of his sons ; he'd said enough ;
No more he'd say, except may God *preserve*
The valiant fellows who so well deserve ;
Although his boys were *absent*, he'd no doubt
Of putting all the robbers to the rout,
Who, of the *sweets* of life the settlers rifle,
And leave untouched not e'en the smallest *trifle* ;
He hoped to stop their long career of vice,
And see their carcases as cold as *ice* ;
Said he, the *fruits* of all their deeds, I tell ye,
Shall be, we'll beat the rascals to a *jelly*.

A Tinker rose and said, that with *clean hands*,
Thank God, he volunteered to fight those bands
Of armed banditti which infest this spot,
And hoped they all would soon be sent to *pot* ;
Rogues, that for murder and for rapine lurk,
His *honor* shrunk from all such *dirty* work !
T'were better soon from out the world to send them,
Because he thought them too far gone to *mend them.*

A *Hatter* rising made a warm oration ;
He said he *felt* such mighty trepidation
At hearing all the robbers wanton sins,
That for the world he'd not be in their *skins* ;
With all his heart he'd join against the *band*,
And vowed success must *crown* each gallant hand,
For he'd be *bound*, they'd nothing more to do
But find the villains, and then *buckle* to ;
In short, he saw the rogues had cause for quaking,
For they were on the *verge* of being taken,
That like the *Beaver*, they would hunt them *down*,
And bring them *flayed* like *rabbits* into town ;
We'll shew the Gov'nor and the soldiers here,
What men can do who're destitute of fear !

The Parson's Clerk then rose with speech most witty,
Hoping they'd kill the rascally banditti ;

As for himself, (to chose the least of evil,)
He'd stay in Launceston and *fight the devil* !

The Tailor rose, and called the Clerk a lout,
And begged the gentlemen would *turn* him out :
To see a *timid man* he could not bear,
He only wished for men of *courage* there ;
The latter speech was scarcely uttered, when
The Clerk walked out, and going, said *Amen.*


# End of the First Canto.

# CONTENTS

### OF THE

## Second Canto.

---

*An argument as to who should be captain of the volunteers. — Each modestly proposes himself as leader, and relates his valorous deeds in support of his qualification. — The Tailor's feat being considered the most gallant — he is unanimously chosen captain. — They go in pursuit of the banditti. — Their forgetfulness — Captain Snip's mistake.— The Grocer's Apprentice and the Baker puzzled. — The Cobbler's joy at Captain Snip's mistake .— The volunteers return home, and supply themselves with ammunition. — They march again, and at length see the supposed robbers sleeping beneath a tree. — Their gallant conduct on the occasion.*

# Canto Second.

The noble heroes now had proudly each
Made a magnanimous and warlike speech,
When Io ! an argument remained in store,
Who should be captain of their valient corps !
Each man most modestly proposed that he,
Should lead the others on to victory ;
Vast were the tales recounted by each one,
Of noble deeds that he himself had done.
*This*, on a hay-stack, winged a small tom-tit,
And if that he so small a thing could hit,
Why sure the only inference was then,
That he was qualified to shoot at *men.*
In fact he had no doubt, upon his word,
He should next shot have *nearly* killed the bird,
But he was forced against his own desire
To *run*, because he'ad set the *stack on fire !*

Another, passing by a flock of geese,
The birds attacked him, and he fired his piece,
And put them *all to flight*, though on the spot
His pig unluckily received he shot,

Which shows how dangerous it is to be
Mixing one's self in bad society.

*One* vowed, and firmly swore, upon his soul
He one day saw a rat within its hole,
And (being bless'd with nerve and courage stout),
He seized its tail, and pulled the vermin out !
And if he thus could act in such a case,
Could he not pull from out their lurking place
The lawless gang, just like so many rats,
And make them food for hungry dogs and cats !

The *Tailor* said he had to boast what few
In that assembly he believed could do,
He'ad beat two men till they were black and blue,
In short like ninepins he had knocked them down,
Which he could prove, by twenty men in town ;
He mauled them so in this most gallant fray,
That they most gladly would have *ran away*,
But (to their cost) they could not stir a peg,
For *both* the scoundrels had a *wooden leg* !

Another proved that once in mortal rage,
He thrashed his grandsire, though *five times his age*,
For seventy-five revolving years he'd seen,
And he (himself) was only just fifteen !
And when his grannam interfered, why lo !

His spirit kindled. and he *thrashed her too !*

The others' feats my muse disdains to name,
Because she deems they cannot justly claim
The smallest title to renown or fame.
At last they all with one accord agreed,
The *Tailor's* action was the bravest deed,
And each resolved to make this daring trip
Under the charge of gallant *Captain Snip,*
Who proudly—fiercely girding on *his shears,*
Exclaimed come on, I'll clip the villains' ears !
Another moon shall never pass away
Ere Brady's gang return to mother clay !
As mine's the task to lead you on to fame,
I'll prove me worthy of a captain's name !
Beat, beat to arms ! let every hero come !
With that the *Tinker* beat his *kettle-drum !*
Now in pursuit they onward bend their way,
And walk full half the tedious sultry day
O'er lofty hills, before they luckless find,
That every *bullet* had been *left behind !*
That Captain Snip by some mistake, good lack,
(Instead of powder) gave them all *lamp black !*
Well might the Grocer's little 'prentice puzzle
To find the cause (*though loaded to the muzzle !*)
His gun would not go off and shoot,

That noble animal—the *bandicoot* !

Well might the wond'ring *Baker* try
To ascertain the reason why
His gun so obstinate refused to fire,
And gratify his murderous desire ;
Because if *real* powder had been used,
The musket would have still refused
To breathe destruction to the kang'roo-rat,
Which on a log most impudently sat,
Nor seemed inclined to stir a single jot,
As though it knew the baker's gun had got
It's charge of powder placed *above the shot* !
Well might the *Cobbler* joyous feel,
And wilh thanksgiving grateful kneel,
For Captain Snip's most fortunate mistake,
Made, as it were, on purpose for his sake ;
For had the *Tinker* hapless shot him dead,
When thrice he took his black and brushy head
(Behind a tree) to be a large oppossum,
The *cobbling* trade had lost its brightest blossom.

And now returning, with all expedition,
They quick obtain some *real* ammuuition,
And march again, provided with a sack,
To bring the heads of all the robbers back ;

For many a mile, through many a sultry day,
In vain these heroes o'er the mountains stray,
When fortune deeming it was monstrous hard.
That men so spirited should be debarred
From falling in with Brady's treacherous crew,
And proving what a valorous heart could do,
Made the keen eyes of all the party see
The looked-for robbers sleeping 'neath a tree ;
Gladly they saw the rascals *snoring lay,*
Then fixed their bayonets and — *ran away.*

**End of the Second Canto.**

# CONTENTS

OF THE

# 𝕿𝖍𝖎𝖗𝖉 𝕮𝖆𝖓𝖙𝖔.

Captain Snip's speech — his excuse for running away the first — The volunteers rally their spirits, return to the charge, and fire upon the sleeping party, but without effect.— The volunteers challenged by two men.— Each party takes the other for bush-rangers. — The volunteers surrender their arms to the two strangers, who afterwards prove to be soldiers of the 40th Regiment.— The prisoners examined before a Magistrate and discharged..— His Worship expresses great satisfaction at the conduct of the soldiers, and makes every allowance for their mistake.— The volunteers surprised by Brady's gang, and taken prisoners.— Captain Snip's extreme alarm and agitation.— His excuse for bearing arms.— Brady convicts him of lying — sentences them to die—gives them ten minutes to confess their crimes, and make their peace with Heaven.— The robbers astonished at their confessions.— The sentence of death commuted to flagellation.— The punishment inflicted.— Brady facetiously compares himself to a musician.— Dismisses his prisoners in dishabille.— Their arrival in Launceston in that condition.

# Canto Third.

Now when they ceased to urge the timorous flight,
And those who fainted through th' excessive fright
Had well recovered, thus their captain spake :
" My friends, reflection says t'was wrong to make
" At such a time this needless hasty flight,
" Before occasion had been given for fright ;
" That I ran *first*, I really don't deny,
" But t'was not fear, like yours, that made me fly ;
" Ah, no ! a very different cause indeed,
" Believe me, Gentlemen, had urged *my speed* ;
" I ran (to make your capture quite complete)
" I hopes of cutting off the knaves retreat !
" Take courage, friends, your flagging spirits rally,
" Our foes are sleeping, let us make a sally —
" The hazy morning favours our attack,
" Come on ! their heads shall quickly fill this sack."
With that they fiercely seize their arms and go,
Resolved to masacre the daring foe ;
Again they view them, and then softly creep,
And fire their muskets at the rogues asleep ;
But kindly harmless every bullet passes,

And spares the lives of five or six *jackasses,*
Which foggy weather, intermixed with fear,
Most wonderfully had made appear
As nothing less than Brady's lawless clan,
Fast in the arms of Morpheus, to a man !
The startled animals their long ears pricking,
Jumped up, and proved themselves *alive and kick-*
    *ing,*
For, cocking their tails, o'er hill and dale they bound,
Leaving the warriors masters of the ground,
(Except a few who'd shut both eyes to fire,
And did not open either to enquire,
*Before they ran,* how many robbers bled,
Or whether the whole, or only part were dead,
But deemed it prudent quickly to retire,
Lest *unslain* robbers might *return the fire.*

The flying heroes in a scrub concealed,
Soon viewed their comrades masters of the field,
Then (venturing out to join their friends again)
*First* learn their firing had been all in vain.
Scarce had they joined, when lo ! two men appear,
Strangers to them, and strangers too to fear ;
Your arms surrender sternly loud they cry,
Or every rascal of your gang shall die.
No sooner spoke, than down their arms were laid.

First letting all the party understand,
He thought they really did not seem to be
By any means o'erstocked with bravery ;
Then (being dismissed) the *heroes* went their ways,
And thus his Worship gave the soldiers praise ;
My gallant friends, I must allow to you,
There's greatest praise and every credit due,
In spite of your unfortunate mistake,
An error very *natural* to make ;
So *natural* indeed my mind conceives,
The *devil himself* would take them all for *thieves !*

Short was their joy for liberty regained,
When fortune unpropitiously ordained,
Next day that ev'ry volunteer should be,
Again the child of sad captivity.
Alas ! whilst busied setting stitches,
And mending his *company's* ragged breeches,
The unsuspecting Captain Snip descries
(With terror equal to his great surprise)
The daring Brady with his lawless band,
Around himself and hapless comrades stand
With bay'nets fixed ; the robbers loudly cry,
Your arms surrender, or each man shall die !
The mandate uttered, 'twas as soon obeyed ;
When Brady frowning fiercely, stern surveyed

His captive foes, and then demanded why
They should not all that very instant die ?
The arms they yielded, he too plainly knew,
Were solely borne against himself and crew.
When thus to him did Captain Snip reply
With chatt'ring teeth, and tearful sorrowing eye,
Upon his trembling and submissive knees ;
My *Lord*—your *Excellency*—your *Honor*—please
To spare our lives, we're not (as you suppose)
Armed as your *Rev'rence's* most daring foes,
But only *sportsmen* bearing guns to shoot
The *kangaroo-rat* and *bandicoot.*
But most unluckily for Captain Snip,
T'was proved his tongue had made a trifling slip
From truth, because himself and comrades all
(When searched) had nought about themselves but
    *ball.*
Good shots, cried Brady, you must be to shoot
The kangaroo-rat and bandicoot
*With musket balls* — for gem'men you have not
About your persons e'en a *grain of shot.*
But, sirs, I'm not so credulous an ass,
To let your *bandicoot* assertion pass
Upon my mind as real truth, for I
Conceive these bullets prove your tale a lie ;
And therefore sentence every man to die.

But harkee, previous to your decease
Perhaps your consciences would fain make peace
With Heaven, and candidly aloud confess
Your various deeds of shameful wickedness ;
Do so this instant, for I only give
Ten fleeting minutes for each man to live !
Down on their knees, th' affrighted captives fall,
And just like dying thieves, recounted all
The most notorious and shameful crimes,
That they'd been guilty of at various times ;
The wond'ring robbers smiling, said, why then
Compared with these w'are really honest men ;
We in comparison are men of worth
To them the greatest scoundreds upon earth.
Ure wretched pris'ners on their knees remain,
And beg their lives, nor do they sue in vain,
For after some discussion and dispute,
The robbers all determine to commute
The rigid sentence of annihilation,
Into the punishment of *flagellation*
With *cat-o'-nine-tails*, and with one accord,
Most kindly liberally did award
To every *private volunteer*, the sum
Of *fifty lashes* on his naked b—m,
By way of what they called a pay or pension,
Due to their services and good intention,

But as remuneration for his trouble,
They gen'rous gave to Captain Snip full double
The sum or payment that his men received,
Not that h'ad greater services achieved,
But that they thought it was not proper then
To pay an *officer* like *common men*.
The flogging o'er, said Brady (jeering) pray
Don't you consider, Gentlemen, I play
Upon thot instrument the *fiddle* well!
Now prithee be ingenuous and tell
Did not I make the *sounding strings* impart
A *tender feeling*, that subdued the heart?
At least, my friends, it plainly now appears,
I *played so well* it moved you all to tears!
But, Gentlemen, allow me now to say,
When next I chance to undertake to play,
I shall most willingly indeed consent,
T' excuse your *vocal base accomp'niment*.
Now, Gentlemen, be pleased to loose your braces,
And then surrender me your *fiddle cases*,
That is to say, if you will now allow sirs,
I'll take the liberty to take your trowsers!
Then loudly laughing at his quizzing speeches,
Dismissed his prisoners without their *breeches*,
Begging them not their triffling loss deplore,
As Captain Snip could eas'ly *make them more*.

In such a glaring dishabille, alas !
Through streets of Launceston compelled to pass,
The girls and women vowed t'was monstrous rude
For men to walk about the town so nude ;
While every ragged little urchin screeches,
Pray what's the price of buck-*skin* breeches ?
At last they gladly each arrive once more
Safely within his own respective door,
Resolved no more in search of fame to roam
To mind his business, and stay at home.

## End of the Third Canto.

PRINTED BY A. BENT, COLONIAL TIMES OFFICE.

# END NOTES

## Michael Howe

1. See *Historical Records of Australia*, Series III., Vol. II., p. 387 and Note 148.
2. See *Historical Records of Australia*, Series I., Vol. VIII., pp.202 and 264, where the Proclamation is printed in full.
3. See West, *History of Tasmania*, Vol. II., p. 130.
4. See *Historical Records of Australia*, Series III., Vol. II., p. 576 and Note 201.
5. See *Historical Records of Australia*, Series III., Vol. II., pp. 16, 194, 634 and notes
6. See *Historical Records of Australia*, Vol. III., Part II. P.194 and Note 85.
7. See *Historical Records of Australia*, Series III ., Vol. 11., pp 275, 294.

Michael Howe, drawn by Aidan Phelan.

# Matthew Brady

1.      For the extraordinary career of Alexander Pearce, who absconded from Macquarie Harbour in 1822, see The Hobart Town Gazette for 1824, and West, History of Tasmania, Vol. II., page 197 and note.

2.      West, *History of Tasmania*. Vol. II., p. 200.

3.      McCabe, shot through the hand by Brady for offering violence to a woman, was then flogged and expelled from the gang. Soon afterwards he was caught by the police, tried and within ten days executed.

4.      As compensation for his injury, Gunn later received from the colonists an address of thanks, and from the Colonial Fund a pension of £70 per annum and a position as Superintendent of Hobart Town Prisoners' Barracks.

5.      Lieutenant William Henry Breton, in his *Excursions in New South Wales. Western Australia and Van Diemen's Land, during the years 1830, 1832, 1832 and 1833*. London, 1834, pp. 335 et seq.

6.      See West, *History of Tasmania*, Vol. II., p. 206.

7.      See Ferguson, *Bibliography of Australia*, No. 1157, p. 425

8.      See *Australian Literature*, Vol. I., page 228

# ALSO IN THIS SERIES FROM ETT IMPRINT

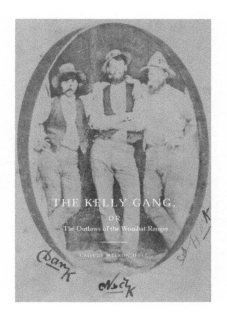

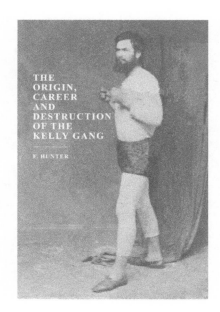

Illustrated reprints of Australian Classics

Printed in Australia
AUHW022357130222
359556AU00008B/21